the MARY KAY WAY

the
MARY KAY WAY

TIMELESS PRINCIPLES FROM AMERICA'S GREATEST WOMAN ENTREPRENEUR

MARY KAY ASH

WILEY

John Wiley & Sons, Inc.

Published by John Wiley & Sons, Inc., Hoboken, New Jersey
Published simultaneously in Canada

For general information on our other products and services or for technical support, please contact our Customer Care Department within the United States at (800) 762-2974, outside the United States at (317) 572-3993 or fax (317) 572-4002.

Wiley also publishes its books in a variety of electronic formats. Some content that appears in print may not be available in electronic books. For more information about Wiley products, visit our web site at www.wiley.com.

Library of Congress Cataloging-in-Publication Data:

Ash, Mary Kay.
   The Mary Kay way: timeless principles from America's greatest woman entrepreneur/ Mary Kay Ash, with Yvonne Pendleton.
       p.   cm.
   ISBN 978-0-470-37995-0   (cloth)
   1. Management.   2. Success in business.   3. Ash, Mary Kay.
I. Pendleton, Yvonne.   II. Title.
HD31.A74   2008
658–dc22   2008012239

Printed in the United States of America.

10 9 8 7 6 5 4 3 2 1

ACKNOWLEDGMENTS

Mary Kay dedicated the original version of this book to "all those who still believe that *people* and *pride* are the two foremost assets in building a successful business."

This new book is dedicated to all those *people* at the Company and in the independent sales force who have helped—with great *pride*—to forge a successful corporation and millions of small businesses around the world according to *The Mary Kay Way.*

—YVONNE PENDLETON

Executive Editor

CONTENTS

THE MARY KAY WAY

This book is the life's work of an extraordinary woman I had the great fortune to call "Grandmother Mary Kay." She lived her life by these principles and philosophies, and raised her family by them. Now that I'm older I can clearly see how she was teaching them to me throughout my childhood. She knew they would make a difference in my life.

In 1963, when she began her "dream company," she adopted the values that shaped her business. Over the course of the past 45 years, they've changed millions of lives for the better within our independent sales force. And they're still the guiding beacons we use to manage the business today. They always will be. My grandmother started it, my father nourished it, and I will perpetuate it; it's The Mary Kay Way.

Grandmother Mary Kay had already received the Hall of Fame Award in the Direct Selling Industry by the time I was born. And at the age of one, I was too young to understand what it meant for her to be selected a Horatio Alger Distinguished American Citizen. At age two, I was still too young to remember when she was profiled on 60 Minutes—the interview where Morley Safer asked, " . . . don't you think in a sense you're using God?" To which Mary Kay replied, "I hope not. I sincerely hope not. I hope He's using me instead." But I do recall how important she always made me feel. As the years passed, I began to understand how much importance Mary Kay placed on the art of listening, on treating people like she would want to be treated, on doing well by doing good. She practiced all these things on her family as well as everyone she did business with.

I was seven years old when this book was first published in 1984 and she autographed a copy for me. I still have it and treasure it because the words in the book ring so true with what I saw in her life. She said, "Learn all of this to use when *you* are <u>President</u> of Mary Kay."

Twenty-four years later, I'm still heeding her advice. This book is something all of us in leadership at Mary Kay Inc. refer to constantly—not only for how to do things *The Mary Kay Way*, but also, as she shares in the introduction, so that we continue to exercise a "sensitivity for the needs of others." I always knew who my grandmother was, and what she did, but it wasn't until after I joined Mary Kay Inc. in 2000 that I began to fully appreciate how much she had meant to so many others. At our headquarters, I would see candid photos of my grandmother—like precious family—framed prominently on people's desks in their offices and cubicles. As I attended Company events with our independent sales force, they would relate their most treasured stories and memories about Mary Kay. At the time of her death, I witnessed firsthand the great outpouring of love for my grandmother. The heartfelt thoughts, the letters, and interviews deepened my sense of how much she had contributed.

Several years ago we hosted, for the first time, a global business conference in Dallas for all the leaders of our Mary Kay subsidiaries around the world. I'll never forget one of our executives holding up a copy of this book and asking the group if everyone had read it.

To those who raised their hands indicating yes, he said, "Great. Read it again."

To the ones who hadn't yet read it, he said, "Get a copy before you leave. Read it." Then he went on to say, "If you find you can't or don't agree with the principles in this book, just go ahead and find the door."

As I began traveling to our world markets, to places like China, Mexico, and Russia, I was surprised to find how well people understood the Mary Kay principles. It didn't matter where I was, there were people practicing *The Mary Kay Way*, making others feel important, and treating others they way they would want to be treated. I would come home and marvel to my dad, Richard Rogers, who helped grandmother start the company, that the Mary Kay culture is an amazing international language. It works everywhere.

Today women who live in countries where my grandmother never traveled are building Mary Kay businesses based on her beliefs. The anecdotal evidence of the difference Mary Kay made in so many lives can at times be downright humbling. Whether it's a woman in Russia who told me she thought her life was over when she was widowed at a young age, an Asian scientist who grappled with giving up a promising career to sell cosmetics, an American woman who grew up in foster care thinking no one cared about her, or a woman in Mexico who sold chickens in the marketplace until finding a better way to feed her family—the life-changing experiences of these women confirm to me that my grandmother had it right.

In 2003, two years after my grandmother's death, I was honored to accept an award accorded her as a result of an academic study by Baylor University to determine the Greatest Entrepreneurs in American History. Henry Ford's great-grandson accepted his award; the late John H. Johnson was there to accept his as Greatest Minority Entrepreneur; and Mary Kay Ash was named Greatest Female Entrepreneur in American History. I said then that the greatest thing my grandmother did for the world was to tap into the minds and hearts of its women.

In 2004 my dad was interviewed by the Wharton School of Business at the University of Pennsylvania after Mary Kay had been named one of the 25 greatest business leaders of our time in a Wharton/PBS study. This book, *Lasting Leadership*, was notable as one of the few times since her death that my father has spoken publicly about my grandmother, whom he had worked with from the age of 20 to build her Company. In a book filled with 23 stories of male leaders like Grove, Gates, Buffett, Walton, Greenspan, and Welch, my Dad talked about one of only two women in the book. He explained how at Mary Kay "relationship building is ingrained as a business model." Nothing illustrates the power of her legacy to build relationships better than our sales force of 1.8 million.

We decided, as this new edition was being planned to celebrate our 45th anniversary, that it would be interesting to add new material showing how the principles in the book have affected the 500 women leaders around the world who used them to build the most successful of Mary Kay businesses—the Independent National Sales Directors. This group cuts across every generation, as well as background, language, and culture. Some have advanced degrees, and some had never worked outside the home prior to Mary Kay.

If there is one thing they agree upon wholeheartedly, it is that these words of Mary Kay Ash are timeless. They say Grandmother's principles resonate magnificently in building a business, in building a life. As they responded to our questions about the significance of this book for them, they urged us to teach these principles to future generations of Mary Kay leaders in the independent sales force and at the Company.

As much as any time in our history, *The Mary Kay Way* governs and fuels our global enterprise as it works to better the lives of untold millions of families around the world. And, it will continue.

—RYAN ROGERS

EDITOR'S PREFACE

When Mary Kay Ash first published this book in 1984, her cosmetics company had recently celebrated its 20th anniversary. She described annual sales exceeding $300 million and an independent sales force of more than 200,000. This new edition comes at the 45th anniversary, with wholesale sales exceeding $2.4 billion and a worldwide independent sales force of 1.8 million. Mary Kay® consistently ranks among the top U.S. brands. We at Mary Kay Inc. are very proud of her legacy and excited to share it with you in this new edition of her most important book. The principles in this book are the foundation for everything we do, and are responsible for the dramatic growth of the business and its worldwide reputation in the years since Mary Kay Ash founded what she called her "dream" company in 1963.

We know that the Mary Kay culture is respected in business circles, and that it is studied at some of the most prestigious academic institutions.

Recently, we asked Mary Kay's Independent National Sales Directors, the highest-achieving women in the sales force, to share principles from this book that had the most profound impact on their businesses and their lives. One hundred seventy-five of them, from throughout the world, eagerly responded. As their comments were translated and collated, a consensus emerged. All of these remarkable women believed this book to be instrumental in their success. Today, they teach from it, make speeches centered upon it, and discuss leadership examples with their vastly diverse teams based on these principles. They also continue to be inspired by the messages. Many suggest *The Mary Kay Way be mandatory reading for anyone aspiring to build and be successful in a business. All endorse it as the way to build a life. As National Sales Director Svetlana Kisurkina of Ukraine said, "I know for sure that in critical moments I can find in this book answers for all my questions."*

For one National Sales Director in the United States, it had been a few years since she'd picked up her beloved, dog-eared copy of the first edition of this book. Sherril Steinman took the occasion of responding to the survey to reread it from cover-to-cover. Upon completing it, she did three things. In her words:

1. *I cried and cried at the genius of Mary Kay Ash.*
2. *I called the leader of the sales group at the Company and suggested we make this mandatory reading for everyone.*
3. *I wrote a letter to Helen McVoy [one of the first two women ever to become a National Sales Director in 1971] to express to her my gratitude for everything she taught me and for being the role model I wanted to emulate in my work.*

Many among the National Sales Directors had the extraordinary experience of working alongside Mary Kay Ash. But whether they learned of her wisdom firsthand or through a mentor, all of them have taken Mary Kay's philosophies to heart. They speak convincingly about perpetuating Mary Kay principles for future generations, as the company founder introduced them.

INTRODUCTION

Most books on leadership have been written *by* men—and *for* men. Although I believe women can learn a great deal from such books, I also believe it isn't possible for us to clone ourselves from our male counterparts, because *we are different*. Women can no more duplicate the male style of management than American businessmen can exactly reproduce the Japanese style. This is not to suggest that Americans and Japanese cannot learn from one another—they can and do. Similarly women can gain considerable leadership know-how from men. By the same token, men can also learn much from women. To me, P and L doesn't only mean profit and loss—it also means *people* and *love*.

People come first at Mary Kay—independent sales force employees, consumers, and our suppliers. We pride ourselves as a "company known for the people it *keeps*." Our belief in caring for people, however, does not conflict with our need as a corporation to generate a profit. Yes, we keep our eye on the bottom line, but it's not an overriding obsession.

Many view us as an enigma, but the Mary Kay success story is no mystery to me. This remarkable Company and independent sales force have succeeded not through "dog eat dog" competition so commonplace in "big business," but through sensitivity for the needs of others. We could never have grown to where we are today without the enthusiasm of thousands of women and a committed staff. Our secret is a unique leadership concept, based on the Golden Rule, that allows fairness to flourish in business. Our methods are applicable to any organization, and the purpose of this book is to share them with you now.

My story begins with what others may regard as a conclusion. In 1963, before starting my own company, I retired after twenty-five years in direct sales. I loved my work, and as national Training Director of a large corporation I had achieved many of my goals, but as I reflected upon my career I was still disheartened.

The boredom of retirement caused a deepening sense of discontent. I had achieved success, but I felt that my hard work and abilities had never been justly rewarded. I knew I had been denied opportunities to fulfill my potential simply because I was a woman, and I was certain these feelings were not mere indulgences of self-pity, because I had personally known so many other women who suffered similar injustices.

I also knew that repressed anger was unhealthy. For years I had prided myself on being a positive person, and here I was—full of negative thoughts. To ward off those feelings, I decided to make a list of all the good things that had happened to me during the previous twenty-five years. Forcing myself to think positively did wonders for my spirit. I was able to overcome the discontent inside me, and my old enthusiasm slowly returned. Suddenly it occurred to me that these notes might serve as the basis for a book aimed at helping others. So I went deeper, and listed all the problems I felt had hindered my career.

I read through those lists again and again, convinced I was on to something. As a mother strives to protect her children, I wanted to help other women so they wouldn't have to suffer what I had endured. I realized that those lists were evolving into a how-to book about the right way to lead and motivate people. But who was I to write a book on leadership? I had no formal credentials in that area, or as an author. No matter how effective my ideas were, who would pay attention to them? Nevertheless, the Golden Rule— "Do unto others as you would have them do unto you"— kept racing through my mind. If I had been in charge of my old company, that's the rule I would have used with all people—men and women alike. It seemed to me that following the Golden Rule was such an obvious way to motivate and lead.

If such a company did exist, I reasoned, then it would surely be a "dream company." Instantly a bold but simple question emerged: "Instead of just talking or writing about it—why don't you actually do it?" That was when I decided to fulfill the dream.

Once I made that decision, I needed something to sell. I wanted a top-quality product—one that could benefit other women, and one that women would be comfortable selling. I also wanted to offer women an open-ended opportunity to do anything they were smart enough, and motivated enough, to do.

After spending days and nights trying to think of such a product, it finally dawned on me one evening while I was getting ready for bed—my skin care products. I had been introduced to them 10 years earlier by a local cosmetologist I had called on during my direct-selling days. Using formulas created by her dad, she developed creams and lotions for customers of her small, home-operated beauty shop. In additional to myself, many of my relatives and friends had been using these wonderful products for several years, so when the cosmetologist died, I bought the original formulas from her family. From my own use and the results I had personally received, I knew that these skin care products were tremendous; with some modifications and high-quality packaging, I was sure they would be big sellers!

Although our Company now includes men's products, my main objective was to establish a company that would give unlimited opportunity to women. It was a period when women were often paid fifty cents on the dollar that men received for the same work. It disturbed me that men were paid more "because they had families to support." It also disturbed me whenever a male manager put down one of my new ideas or suggestions with, "Mary Kay, you're thinking just like a woman."

Throughout this book I discuss the specific ways in which women *do* think differently from men. Such differences are in no way inferior to or incompatible with "the way a man thinks." And so one of my objectives in founding Mary Kay was to create a business atmosphere in which "thinking like a woman" would not be a liability. In my Company those special sensitivities and talents often labeled "women's intuition" would be nurtured – not stifled.

Unlike many people who start a new business, money was not my prime motivation—not that I was so well off that it wasn't a consideration; in fact, I had put my lifetime savings on the line. The business had to succeed or I would never have another opportunity to start my own business.

On Friday, September 13, 1963, I opened the doors to Mary Kay Cosmetics in a 500-square-foot store front in Dallas. My twenty-year-old son, Richard, joined me, and nine enthusiastic women became the first Mary Kay Independent Beauty Consultants. All of us worked side-by-side. There were no job descriptions. We all did whatever needed to be done. I sold, taught other women, conducted sales meetings, and emptied wastebaskets.

Richard did the bookkeeping and filled orders. Over the years we grew steadily, adhering to our original decision to operate the business according to the Golden Rule and to offer unlimited opportunities to women.

Today, as founder and chairman of Mary Kay, I'm finally writing the book on leadership that was begun in 1963. What was theory is now fact. We now have twenty years of successful experience. This book is especially intended for those millions of women who have entered the job market.

When we started in business, it was easy to operate like a caring family. There were only a few of us, each dependent on the others. We cared about each other and worked side-by-side as equals. Now that we're big, it's not quite as easy to maintain a family atmosphere. Not easy, but not impossible either. We work hard at it constantly, giving it top priority. And it works.

the MARY KAY WAY

1 Golden Rule Leadership

The Golden Rule teaches us to "Do unto others as we would have others do unto us." The Bible tells us this in the Book of Matthew (7:12), and this message is just as meaningful today as ever. Of course, it was meant for everyone, but what a perfect rule of conduct for leadership!

Unfortunately many people today consider the Golden Rule a tiresome cliché, but it still is the best key to leadership. At Mary Kay Inc. we take it very seriously. Every leadership decision made is based on the Golden Rule.

Following the Golden Rule Can Bring Success

When I first sat down to write a book about the way I thought a company should work, I wanted to provide a guide for leaders that would serve as a model for working with *people*. Being a mother and grandmother, my maternal instinct made me want to do for my associates what every mother wants to do for her children— what's best for them.

I had spent many years working for somebody else, so I knew firsthand what it was like to be accountable to another person.

Beginning my own business and being determined to implement a leadership style that would engender enthusiasm, I vowed that my company would never repeat the wrongs that I had witnessed in other companies for which I had worked. People would be treated fairly; I would always think, "If I were this person, how would I want to be treated?" To this day, when I am searching for a solution to a people problem, I ask myself that question. And when I do, even the most difficult problem soon becomes unraveled.

Many of the unpleasant experiences in my previous career taught me the rules for dealing with people. I can remember once spending ten days on a round-trip bus ride from Texas to Massachusetts with fifty-seven other salespeople on a home-office pilgrimage that was to be our reward for being sales leaders. It was a horrendous trip with several bus breakdowns, but we were willing to endure it for the pot of gold at the end of the rainbow: Meeting the president of the company as guests in his home.

But instead we were given a tour of the plant. Now, a manufacturing plant can be very interesting and a nice place to work—ours is. But I was there to meet the president. When we were finally invited to the president's home, we were only allowed to walk through his rose garden, and we never even had an opportunity to meet with him personally. What a letdown! Needless to say, it was a very long and quiet bus trip back to Texas for all fifty-eight of us.

Another time, I was attending an all-day sales seminar and was anxious to shake hands with our sales manager, who had delivered an inspiring speech. After waiting in line for three hours, it was finally my turn to meet him. He never even looked at me. Instead he looked over my shoulder to see how much longer the line was. He wasn't even aware that he was shaking my hand. And although I realized how tired he must have been, I, too, had been there for three hours and was just as tired! I was hurt and offended because he had treated me as if I didn't even exist. Right on the spot I made a decision that if I ever became someone whom people waited in line to shake hands with, I'd give the person in front of me my undivided attention—no matter how tired I was!

I have been very fortunate. Mary Kay has become a large company, and many times, I've stood at the head of a long reception line for several hours to shake hands with hundreds of people. But no matter how tired I was, I have always made it a point to remember the rejection I felt waiting in that long line to shake hands with that indifferent sales manager. With that in mind, I always look each person squarely in the eyes, and whenever possible, try to say something personal. It might be only a comment such as "I love your hair" or "What a beautiful dress you're wearing," but I give each person my undivided attention, and I don't allow anything to distract me. Each person whose hand I shake is the most important person in the world to me at that moment.

Once every month, a group of Independent Sales Directors comes to Dallas to visit the Company for an educational program. Although as many as 400 women have attended these training sessions at one time, I always spend a portion of a day in class with them. And during their visit, I invite them all to come to my home for tea and cookies—which I personally bake. Time after time I hear, "Mary Kay, I've never eaten a cookie baked by a chairman of the board before." But you see, I never forgot the time when we weren't invited into the president's home, and so I make our people welcome in mine. Evidently it's important for them to see how I live, for they invariably say that the visit to my home was the highlight of the trip. I immensely enjoy their company, and I look forward to each visit. These women are very dear to me.

New Independent Sales Directors continue to come to our Dallas headquarters for a week of education and motivation. They enjoy getting to know women who are taking this important step at the same time, snapping commemorative photos with Company executives and taking turns posing for a photo in a replica of Mary Kay's pink bathtub—a longtime symbol of good luck stemming from the days when Sales Directors lined up to do that in Mary Kay's own home. Cookies made from Mary Kay's original recipes are served. Attendees receive special inspiration from top sales force achievers.

Leaders at the top of the corporate ladder sometimes forget the mistreatment they had to endure before they got there, or what is worse, they try to get even: "My boss never listened to my personal problems, so don't bother me with yours," or "My boss gave me ulcers; now it's my turn to give them to someone else!" Such an attitude only perpetuates someone else's wrongdoings.

There are many stories I could tell you about some of my past experiences. Yet, surprisingly, when I take time to review incident by incident, those managers were not as callous and thoughtless as they might first appear. For the most part they were decent, capable people who sincerely believed they were doing a good job. Their shortcomings were due to a lack of empathy for their associates. They failed to ask themselves that all-important question: *"What would I do if I were the other person?"*

In the Mary Kay independent sales force, an individual can expand and progress without moving "up" a traditional corporate ladder. Millions of Beauty Consultants operate independent retail businesses dealing directly with their customers. Each Independent Beauty Consultant defines her own goals, productivity, and rewards. One expression of this responsibility is the role of Independent Sales

Director. This individual builds a team, educates, and guides other Beauty Consultants.

The Adoptee Program

One of the first things I wanted my dream company to eliminate was assigned territories. I had worked for several direct-sales organizations in the past, and I knew how unfairly I had been treated when I had to move from Houston to St. Louis because of my husband's new job. I had been making $1,000 a month in commissions from the Houston sales unit that I had built over a period of eight years, and I lost it all when I moved. I felt that it wasn't fair for someone else to inherit those Houston salespeople whom I had worked so hard to build and educate.

Because we don't have territories at Mary Kay, an Independent Sales Director who lives in Chicago can be vacationing in Florida or visiting a friend in Pittsburgh and gain a new team member while there. It doesn't matter where she lives in the United States; she will always draw a commission from the Company on the retail sales made by that Beauty Consultant. An Independent Sales Director in Pittsburgh will take the visiting Sales Director's new Beauty Consultant under her wing and educate her; the new Beauty Consultant will attend the Pittsburgh unit meetings and participate in local sales contests. Although the Pittsburgh Sales Director will devote a lot of time and effort to the new Beauty Consultant, the Chicago Sales Director will be paid the commissions. We call this our "adoptee" program.

Today we have thousands of Sales Directors, and most of them educate and motivate people in their units who live outside their home states. Some have Beauty Consultants in a dozen or more states. Outsiders look at our company and say, "Your adoptee program can't possibly work!" But it does work. Each Sales Director reaps the benefits from her unit members in other cities and helps other units' members in return.

"But why should anybody work to develop an adoptee—and never receive a commission on her sales?" people from other companies ask. "Why should *I* work to move *your* team member up the ladder of success, so *you* can get all the commissions? What's in it for me?" they say. At Mary Kay, however, many Sales Directors who have as many as 100 adoptees don't think that way. Instead they think, "I'm helping them, but someone else is helping *my* unit members in another city." The system works, and as far as I know, no other company has one quite like ours. But it's a system that a company must institute right from the beginning. I don't think an adoptee program would work if a company attempted to install it years after it was founded.

When we began our adoptee program, it was generally felt that it wouldn't work. But I *knew* it would. I knew it would work because it was based on the Golden Rule. At Mary Kay we sometimes call it the Go-Give® principle. It's a philosophy based on *giving*, and it is applied in every aspect of our business.

Giving more than you expect to receive is what the Go-Give® spirit is all about. Each month, an independent sales force member who embodies this spirit is selected by her peers for a monthly Go-Give® Award. One of those monthly winners is later presented with the Annual Go-Give® Award. Because this achievement was held in the highest regard by Mary Kay herself, the Annual Go-Give® Award is considered the most honorable of all independent sales force recognitions and deeply cherished throughout the world by those who earn it.

While I know that our adoptee program is not applicable to every business, it does serve as a model for any leader wishing to institute a "help others" philosophy. Good leaders should never have dollar signs in their eyes, regarding people merely in terms of profit. An attitude such as ours must permeate an entire organization from top management right on down to the consumer. When everybody is motivated to serve others, everybody benefits.

When it comes to our sales approach we do not like a Beauty Consultant to think, "How much can I sell these women?" Instead we stress, "What can I do to make these women leave here today feeling better about themselves? How can I help them have a better self-image?" Our thinking is that if a woman feels attractive on the outside, she becomes attractive on the inside too.

I know what it's like to spend an entire day in the field and come home without a single order. And I understand the feelings a Sales Director has when she has spent weeks of love and care training a new unit member only to have that person quit before she even starts. Along the way, I've had my share of disappointments in the business. In fact, after having spent 45 years in direct sales, I've experienced most of the problems anyone can think of. While some managers try to forget problems they encountered early in their careers, I make a conscious effort to remember the difficulties I've had along the way. I think it's vital for a leader to empathize with the other person's problem, and the best way to have a clear understanding is to have been there yourself!

At Mary Kay, Beauty Consultants receive guidance and leadership from Sales Directors. Every woman enters our business as a Beauty Consultant, so by the time she becomes a Sales Director she is thoroughly familiar with the trials and tribulations that are encountered in the field. As part of our educational program we teach each Sales Director to ask herself, "If I were in her position and she were in mine, how would I solve the problem?" With this "double vision," good leaders will deal far more successfully with problems than those who insist upon wearing only their supervisor's hat.

Treat People Fairly

Solving management problems by applying the Golden Rule
means treating people fairly and according to merit, not merely
using them for self-serving purposes. To some this seems in
conflict with a company's profit motive; I think, however, the two
can be harmonious. For instance, a person may ask for an unrea-
sonably high increase in salary, one that does not give the company
a fair return for services rendered. "My wife lost her job, and we
have two kids in college," an employee may plead. "I need a raise."
A good leader will be sympathetic, but he can't always comply with
even the most justifiable wants and needs of his employees. In
order to balance responsibilities to the company, the employee,
and all other employees, every leader must be able to say no.

I understand that this can be unpleasant. But instead of
approaching the job as a task to be endured, I try to turn it into a
positive situation. I want that employee to turn a "no" into the
motivation for accomplishing more. And I do this with four
simple steps.

1. It is imperative that each employee be confident that no deci-
    sion will be arbitrary. And so the first thing I do is listen and
    then restate the question. This reassures the employee that I
    do indeed understand the scope of the problem.

2. I clearly list the logical reasons why his request cannot be
    granted.

3. I give a direct "no" statement. This is so important if you are
    to build trust and respect among people. It's not fair to expect
    someone else to surmise or guess your real intent.

4. And finally, I try to suggest how the employee's goal may be
    reached by some other path. For example, to this hypothetical
    employee I might say, "Bill, I am truly sorry about your wife's

misfortune. But you know, she may be on the threshold of a whole new career. This could be your opportunity to help her discover her real talents. God didn't have time to make a nobody; we all have the capacity for greatness. Why don't you sit down with her tonight and talk about what she would really like to accomplish next?"

A good leader will confront problems of this nature with sensitivity and seek the best solutions. But the solutions cannot compromise her responsibility to her company or to other people within the organization. Like a loving parent who listens to his child but does not always let him have his way, a leader will strive to treat everyone fairly and give rewards accordingly. Practicing the Golden Rule does not imply that a company is a part-time charitable institution. Nor should it be assumed that an employee can never be terminated or temporarily laid off. Sometimes a leader must perform unpleasant tasks that serve the best interest of the company, but that may disappoint or hurt a subordinate. In these incidences the leader should exercise the utmost gentleness and compassion—there's even a right way to discharge an employee by the Golden Rule.

I know what it means to exist in constant fear of being fired. I once worked with dozens of other women in a huge, open office. The space contained many rows of desks, each back-to-back and side-by-side. It was chaotic trying to work while someone on one side talked on the telephone and someone on the other side called across the room. A giant black and white clock hung above the manager's private office, and every day around 3:30 P.M., the hustle and bustle would come to an abrupt halt. Fear would enter the room. At precisely 4 P.M., "Mr. X" would regularly fire employees. We would all sit around for that last half hour waiting and dreading to see who would "get the ax." If someone was inadvertently called out of the room near the deadly hour, we would hold our breath until she returned to resume her duties and gave us a sign of relief. Often an employee would return in tears and begin cleaning out her desk. Mr. X's method was to fire someone angrily (usually with much yelling), give her an hour to clean out her desk, and presume that she would never again darken his door.

Whenever I encounter an employee who is misplaced in his or her role, I follow a very different procedure. My first move is to counsel this person regarding specific ways he or she could improve. I give suggestions and set reasonable target dates so that he/she may experience an immediate success. But if these efforts fail, I must consider what would be best for both the employee and the company. It has been my experience that when an employee fails, he/she is the most uncomfortable with this fact.

If, for example, I had a public relations employee who simply could not speak before a large audience—a person who lacked the personal energy necessary to inspire others—I would approach the problem with the Golden Rule. How would I feel if I were this employee? I then might say, "Jane, you've been with us for two years, and each time I see you in a public presentation, I know that you are not comfortable. I've watched you suffer through the program as if it were an ordeal. I wish with all my heart that it weren't true, but Jane, I don't believe this is the spot for you. We care about you, and we want you to be successful; is there some other position you would like to try?" If there is no other challenge for her within our company, we will actively help her in obtaining a position with a firm that will more readily utilize her talents. I will not discard an employee as if she were yesterday's newspaper. There are, of course, managers who disagree with this point. Like Mr. X, they maintain that once you discharge someone, he should "pack his bags and go." But on the rare occasion where that situation may be taken advantage of, I would still rather err on the "people side" than err on the "hard-core business side" of this issue.

It must be remembered that not only the company's good health but also its very survival is dependent on its profitability. And while many companies are indeed very philanthropic, the support given to civic and charitable causes is directly contingent upon the ability to operate efficiently as a business.

We not only talk the Golden Rule; we expect everyone to practice it.

As a cornerstone of our culture, we continue to embrace the Golden Rule as a daily guide for business interactions with fellow employees and members of the independent sales force. Individual actions and decisions are based on this timeless philosophy. The Golden Rule has become the Company's mantra for the personalized customer service we routinely expect to provide, and it continues to define not only our culture but also our commitment to excellence in the highly competitive cosmetics industry.

Many years ago a motivational speaker told us of another company that also practiced a philosophy based upon the Golden Rule. He described marbles upon which the Golden Rule had been inscribed. We thought this was most intriguing, a physical representation of our credo. One of the Sales Directors went to the phone and made a call to inquire about the Golden Rule marbles. When she returned to the group, she was incredulous: "Mary Kay, you may not believe this, but the person who initiated the whole idea is a Mary Kay Beauty Consultant!"

Through the years, we have given out thousands of those marbles. When I do so, I say, "I cannot promise you a bed of roses without thorns. Every day problems will come to your door. And when you face those crucial moments, I want you to take this

Golden Rule marble, hold it in your hand, and ask yourself, 'How could I solve this with the Golden Rule? What would Mary Kay do if she were here?'"

While many people think there's no place for the Golden Rule in the business world, at Mary Kay it's part of our business foundation. Furthermore, I don't think effective leadership can be achieved in any other way.

Independent National Sales Directors Talk about Mary Kay Principles in Action Today

"This Golden Rule and correct priorities are not usual in business society of the modern world. But, in my opinion these principles are essential to building a successful Mary Kay business," says Kazakhstan's **Nadezhda Silchenko**. "This is more than principles of ethical conduct; it is a process for spreading good will all around you."

Angie Stoker has been No.1 in Canada for more than five years. "I've found when you apply the Golden Rule to your business associates; you cannot help but build them up. Isn't that what you would expect if the world treated you the way you prefer? I love that I can build people and help them achieve their dreams. Their successes then inspire more people."

Emily McLaughlin of the United States has always emphasized the strong learning culture of Mary Kay. "In today's world of instant communication, it's important to teach patience, understanding, and compassion for others.

That's really what the Golden Rule is all about. Operating this way creates a safe environment for growth. When a person has faith she will always be treated with value, it builds trust within an organization."

"Learning the Golden Rule affected not only my leadership style, but all my lifestyle," says **Larisa Margishvili**, the first to achieve National Sales Director status in Ukraine. She also earned the use of the first pink Mercedes.

Maureen Ledda of the United States believes that the culture developed around Mary Kay's unique adoptee system is "one of the reasons we feel a bond of sisterhood across this nation."

2 You Build with People

No trip to Mary Kay Inc. headquarters in Dallas is complete without touring the unique Mary Kay Museum housed on the ground floor. Not only is it a charming journey through the history of the Company, it's a trip through decades of fashion and beauty trends. One important gallery in the museum features larger-than-life photographs of the Independent National Sales Directors, 500 women around the world who are leaders within the independent sales force. Their prominence in this museum speaks to the important role these women leaders have in the success of the Company. Mary Kay said it best: "We want our message to be, 'We're a people company.'"

A Company Is Only as Good as Its People

In order to grow and progress in the sales force, you don't move upward; you expand outward. This gives the independent sales force a deep sense of personal worth. They know that they are not competing with one another. Therefore the contributions of each individual are of equal value. And when someone—anyone—proposes a new thought, we analyze it, improve upon it, and ultimately, support it with the enthusiasm of a team.

In fact, a company is only as good as its people. Most companies would say that their balance sheets record their most important assets. At Mary Kay, we consider people in the independent sales force and in our corporate offices to be our most important assets. Many corporate executives boast to securities analysts about product lines, new high-rise buildings, and state-of-the-art manufacturing facilities, never once mentioning the people in their organization. While capital assets are essential for growth, people *are* the business. Whenever we meet with analysts, the wonderful people who are associated with our Company are a major topic of our conversation.

When you look at any great business enterprise, you'll find that it's *people* who make it excel. Outstanding businesses are composed of outstanding people. If you have any doubts about that, witness the long list of failures that resulted when acquiring companies replaced existing management with their own executives or when those acquiring companies simply mishandled management, forcing experienced employees to leave of their own accord.

I recall one large conglomerate that bought out a prosperous fast-food chain, fired the management, and replaced them with their own people. Within 18 months, this highly profitable business was operating in the red! What the acquiring company failed to realize was that they weren't buying hundreds of restaurants and equipment. The most valuable asset they purchased was the management team that ran the chain. Without it, the acquisition soon became a costly liability. Dozens of other companies have made similar mistakes.

A company is built with people—remove them, and the company's ability to function effectively is seriously threatened. Today it has become more common for acquiring companies to insist that former managers remain for a certain length of time, and generous performance agreements are often used to induce these experienced managers to continue generating sales and profits. As we say in Texas, "If it ain't broke, don't fix it."

In 1963, I had no previous experience in the cosmetics industry; my forte was recruiting and training salespeople. After I acquired the formulas for the skin care products, the first thing I did was seek out the most reputable cosmetics manufacturer I could find. Specifically, I wanted a firm that not only made quality products, but also observed the U.S. Food and Drug Administration's regulatory requirements to the letter. I knew it would be a fatal mistake to attempt to cut corners. With the right people in charge, we would never have to concern ourselves with that aspect of the business.

When my son Richard joined me, he was a young man with virtually no experience. However, he was very bright, and he realized that whenever a job had to be done that we couldn't do, we could hire an expert to do it. At each point of our growth, we would seek out people with those skills that could strengthen us even more. We built our Company one person at a time. Not only did we find the best cosmetics manufacturer, but also we found people in accounting, law, distribution, and other areas of expertise. And even though marketing had always been my strength, in time, I recognized the need for people with additional talents in this field.

As we grew, we were able to attract the best people to join our staff full time, and we were always willing to pay top dollar for top talent. When it comes to hiring people, a company gets what it pays for. We've also been very competitive in our profit-sharing plan and other benefits we now have. By paying our people generously, we've developed a team of hard-working, efficient employees.

With more than 4,500 employees worldwide, Mary Kay
Inc. and its subsidiaries continue to offer a place where it
is possible to love your job. The impressive percentage of
tenure—more than 45 percent of U.S. employees have at
least 10 years of service–is a source of great pride. From
employee recognition to mentoring, the Mary Kay culture
offers a spirit of encouragement and positive support that
emanates from our Founder. The Mary Kay Ash belief in
balanced priorities, for instance, is a Company value
engendering great loyalty across a diverse workforce.

Good People Are Worth Hanging On To

Of course, it's one thing to attract good people by paying them
well, and it's another thing to train and keep them. At Mary Kay,
a lot of tender loving care is devoted to each person who joins us.
If we spend six months training someone only to see that person
leave us, we feel we have lost a lot of time and money. So once
people come aboard, we make every attempt to keep them. If by
chance they don't seem to be working out in one area, we'll try
our best to find another spot for them. For example, one of my
personal support staff just didn't seem to be right for the job
assignment she had been given. She was a most conscientious person and had been with the Company for four months. She liked
us, and we liked her. After having invested so much time and
money in her, it would have been a shame to lose her (for her sake
as well as ours). We knew there had to be some place in the Company where she'd fit in perfectly. It was just a matter of our making the effort to find it. After sitting down with her and asking a
lot of questions, she was transferred to our accounting

department, where she did a first-rate job. Good people are always hard to find—so when you do find them, it's important to make every effort to keep them!

As Alfred Sloan, one of General Motors' great former CEOs, once said, "Take my assets—but leave me my organization, and in five years, I'll have it all back."

Independent National Sales Directors Talk about Mary Kay Principles in Action Today

Arlene Lenarz had no idea when she left her nursing career to save for college for her four children that she would become one of the top earning Independent National Sales Directors in the United States, earning more than $12 million in commissions during her career. "We don't use people to build our business; we use our business to build people. When you look at any successful business, you see people who make and keep it excellent."

Becoming an independent sales force leader in Mary Kay's first international subsidiary, **Lee Cassidy** of Australia believes Mary Kay's secret is simple: "Simply find out what your people wish to achieve, and then do everything in your power to help them achieve it."

"I learned early from Mary Kay Ash that I should give my career away in order to lead others to success. So I quickly sought to develop those who could move forward," said **Anne Newbury** of the United States, who pioneered for Mary Kay in the New England area, as well as Mexico,

Canada, and Brazil, and broke earnings records in the process.

"This is the most powerful form of development," says **Christina Boyd**, who has persevered in the Philippines, where there are seven thousand islands and more than a hundred dialects. "Helping people realize the insurmountable power that each and every one of us has is my calling. When we show people how to tap into this power, then we become capable of doing the impossible."

3 The Invisible Sign

Every person is special! I sincerely believe this. Each of us wants to feel good about himself or herself, but to me it is just as important to make others feel the same way. Whenever I meet someone, I try to imagine him or her wearing an invisible sign that says: MAKE ME FEEL IMPORTANT! I respond to this sign immediately, and it works wonders.

Some people, however, are so caught up in themselves that they fail to realize that the other person wants to feel important too.

I've already told you how I once waited in a long reception line to shake hands with the company's sales manager, only to have him treat me as if I didn't exist. I'm sure he didn't remember the incident; in fact, he probably was never aware of how much he had hurt me. Yet, after all these years, I still remember—so it obviously had a powerful impact on me. I learned an important lesson about people that day which I have never forgotten: *No matter how busy you are, you must take time to make the other person feel important!*

Many years ago, I wanted to buy a new car. It was at the time when two-toned cars had just been introduced, and I had my heart set on a black and white Ford. Since I never liked to buy what I couldn't afford, I had saved up enough money to pay cash. The car was going to be my birthday present to myself. With money in my purse, off I went to the Ford dealer's showroom.

Obviously the salesman didn't take me seriously. He had seen me drive up in my old car and assumed that I couldn't afford to buy a new one. In those days women couldn't get credit as easily as a man could, so very few of us ever purchased cars for ourselves. We weren't what salesmen considered "live prospects." The Ford representative would hardly give me the time of day. If he was trying to make me feel unimportant, he couldn't have done a better job. At noontime he simply excused himself, saying he was late for a lunch date. I wanted that car in the worst way, so I asked to see the sales manger. But he was out and wouldn't be back until after 1 P.M. So, with time to kill, I decided to take a walk.

Across the street, I strolled into a Mercury dealer's showroom— just to look, for I still intended to buy that black and white Ford. They had a yellow model on the floor, and although I liked it very much, the sticker price was more than I had planned to spend. However, the salesman was so courteous and made me feel as though he really cared about me. When he found out it was my birthday, he excused himself and returned a few minutes later. Fifteen minutes later a secretary brought him a dozen roses, which he handed to me for my birthday. I felt like a million dollars! Needless to say, I bought a yellow Mercury instead of a black and white Ford.

That salesman got the sale because he made me feel important. It didn't matter to him that I was a woman driving an old car. I was a human being, and in his eyes, that meant I was somebody special. He had seen the invisible sign. Every leader should understand that God has planted seeds of greatness in every human being. Each of us is important, and a good leader can bring these seeds to fruition! It's unfortunate that most of us go to our graves with our music still unplayed! It's been said that we use only 10 percent of our God-given ability, and that the other 90 percent is never tapped. Look at Grandma Moses, who started painting at the age of 75. She went on to become a world-renowned artist, but certainly she must have had her talent at an earlier age. Wouldn't it have been a pity if Grandma Moses had never realized her God-given artistic ability?

Make People Feel Important—They Are

I believe every person has the ability to achieve something important, and with that in mind, I regard everyone as special. A manager should feel this way about people, but it's an attitude that can't be faked. You've got to be honestly convinced that every human being is important.

This is a basic lesson, one that you have probably heard many times before. Yet I remind you of it because many business people become so involved in their work that they forget to apply it. "Business is business, Mary Kay," they tell me. "You don't have to treat employees that way. My workers shouldn't expect me to make them feel important. That's not what I'm paid for."

But they're wrong. Making people feel important is precisely what a leader is paid for—because making people feel important motivates them to do better work. It was John D. Rockefeller who said, "I will pay more for the ability to deal with people than for any other commodity under the sun." High morale is a significant factor in increasing productivity, which means that a good leader should continually strive to boost the self-esteem of every individual in his or her organization.

My experience with people is that they generally *do what you expect them to do!* If you expect them to perform well, they will; conversely, if you expect them to perform poorly, they'll probably oblige. I believe that average employees who try their hardest to live up to your high expectations of them will do better than above-average people with low self-esteem. Motivate your people to draw on that untapped 90 percent of their ability, and their level of performance will soar!

How does a leader make people feel important? First, by *listening* to them. Let them know you respect their thinking, and let them voice their opinions. As an added bonus, you might learn something! A friend of mine once told me about an executive of a large retail operation who told one of his branch managers, "There's nothing you could possibly tell me that I haven't already thought about before. Don't ever tell me what you think unless I ask you. Is that understood?" Imagine the loss of self-esteem that branch manager must have felt. It must have taken all the wind out of his sails and adversely affected his performance. When an individual's self-esteem is deflated, his level of energy is decreased. On the other hand, when you make a person feel a great sense of importance, he or she will be walking on cloud nine—and the level of energy will skyrocket.

Responsibility without Authority Can Be Destructive

People also feel important when they're given responsibility. But responsibility without authority can destroy a person's self-esteem. Have you ever noticed a little girl's reaction when she's been given her first baby-sitting assignment with her younger brother? She bubbles with excitement, because she has received the status of a grown-up. But if she is given the responsibility to watch after him, she should also be given the authority to send him to bed early if he misbehaves. That retail executive not only failed to listen to his branch manager, but he stripped him of all authority to make decisions. Consequently, the branch manager developed low self-esteem and left the company for a major competitor. When given authority as well as responsibility in the new job, he began to feel

good about himself and contributed innovative retailing concepts
to his new employer. His contributions were so valuable, in fact,
that he was rapidly promoted to a higher position than his
former boss.

An attorney told me about a meeting his firm conducted for
the officers of a local bank. One of his partners was in charge of
making the arrangements for a luncheon and had sent out for cold
cuts from a nearby deli. The law firm didn't make a very good
impression. Several of the firm's partners complained, so a few
weeks later a female law clerk was given the responsibility, along
with the authority, to arrange a luncheon meeting with another
bank—with a slightly higher budget.

Knowing how important the luncheon was to the firm, the
clerk felt honored to be responsible. She prepared delicious cold
hors d'oeuvres at her home the night before and had some hot
foods delivered from a restaurant in the building. The clerk acted
as hostess, greeting each banker as he or she walked into the firm's
offices. She did a wonderful job because the responsibility of being
in charge of the luncheon made her feel important. The affair
was a huge success. Several notes were received from the bankers
commenting on the lovely luncheon, and shortly thereafter, the
bank began giving some of its law business to the firm.

Let People Know You Appreciate Them

I recommend that you frequently let your people know how much
you appreciate them. I've never yet met a person who didn't want to
be appreciated—and if that's the way you feel, you should express
your appreciation. Even if it's only for showing up for work on
time—let the person know that you value punctuality. "I think it's
great, Jack, that you arrive at the office every morning at 8 A.M.
sharp. I admire people who are punctual." Say that to a worker and

notice how rarely he comes in late thereafter. Or perhaps you like a person's politeness or gentle mannerisms. There has to be something to appreciate in every person—let it be known. Don't keep it a secret!

At Mary Kay we believe in putting Beauty Consultants and Sales Directors on a pedestal. Of all people, I most identify with them, because I spent many years as a salesperson. My attitude of appreciation for them permeates the Company. When independent sales force members visit our world headquarters, for example, we go out of our way to give them the red-carpet treatment. Every person in the Company treats them royally.

As you probably have heard, we offer, based on sales volume, Independent Sales Directors the opportunity to earn the use of pink Cadillacs. To my knowledge, we were the first company to award such a fine automobile to so many people. We chose Cadillacs because they have always epitomized excellence. When a Mary Kay Sales Director drives a pink Cadillac, she is recognized as a person who has done an outstanding job. It signifies that she is very important to our organization. And, of course, once she achieves this important status, she doesn't ever want to relinquish the privilege.

We go first class across the board, and although it's expensive, it's worth it, because our people are made to feel important. For example, each year we take the top Sales Directors and their spouses on deluxe trips, to places such as Hong Kong, Bangkok, London, Paris, Geneva, and Athens. We spare no expense, and although it costs a lot extra per person to fly the Concorde, cruise on the Love Boat, or book suites at the elegant George V in Paris, it is our way of telling them how important they are to our Company. Even in cities that are used to pomp and ceremony, we attract considerable attention. People in the streets stop to watch our beautiful women being escorted from the hotel to limousines, wondering who they are. Those women feel like royalty, and to us, they are!

From the beginning, we have always believed in going first class with our people. If something is too expensive, we'd rather forget it than economize. For instance, we might settle for one elegant banquet a year instead of two moderate ones. Why do we do it this way? Well, think of the feeling of importance you get from dining at a first-rate restaurant. Everything is perfectly done—the cordial greeting of the maitre d', the exquisitely prepared food, everything—and it gives you a sense of satisfaction not experienced in a less elegant establishment.

Just as a fine restaurant extends itself to make its customers feel special, we do everything we can to make our people feel the same way. And if they don't, we're not doing our job. I think it's essential that every leader remember that invisible sign: MAKE ME FEEL IMPORTANT!

Independent National Sales Directors Talk about Mary Kay Principles in Action Today

"Learning to see that every person is a special being makes a leader develop an inner door that generates a special charisma. This, in turn, generates a deep link with the team—developing credibility, faithfulness, and trust among them for a committed team," says **Beatriz Casartelli** of Argentina.

And how, precisely, did Mary Kay Ash use this sign? Three examples of many shared:

"When any of us spoke at an event, she would be listening on the side of the stage. Her arms would be open as we came off the stage. Knowing my words were important enough for her to stand and listen to them amazed me. As a result, when my people teach, speak, or coach, I give them my full attention because it meant so much to me that Mary Kay did that for me," said **Brenda Segal** of the United States.

"As a brand-new Independent Sales Director, I flew to Dallas for an educational event. When checking in at my hotel, they said I had a message. They handed me a beautiful rose and a personal, handwritten note from Mary Kay, which said, 'I'm looking forward to seeing you at my home on Wednesday.' I'll never forget how I felt. It still gives me goose bumps," said **Debbie Mattinson** of Canada.

"Many of us always believed that we should conduct skin care classes and every part of our business as if Mary Kay was in the back of the room watching. You can imagine my surprise, after conducting one of the first skin care classes the year Mary Kay opened in the United Kingdom," says **Martha Langford** of the United States, "that Mary Kay was in attendance and had been observing from backstage. As I walked off stage, she greeted me with these words, 'Martha, I would have bought everything you had to sell! It was a beautiful class.'"

4 Praise People to Success

I believe praise is the best way for a leader to motivate people. At Mary Kay we think praise is so important that our entire marketing plan is based upon it.

For most women, the last bit of applause they received was when they graduated from high school or college. Sometimes it seems that the only women who are applauded are beauty queens and movie stars. A woman could work day and night caring for her family, and the only time she's likely to hear a comment is if she *stops* doing it!

Little Successes Pave the Way to Bigger Successes

Giving praise is deeply embedded in the Mary Kay marketing philosophy, and we're quick to give it at every opportunity. In fact, we begin when someone becomes a new Beauty Consultant. At a skin care class, after a woman has had a facial, the Beauty Consultant asks the guests to comment on each other's improvement. Not only do the women look better; they feel better too—inside and outside! When a woman feels good about herself, it not only generates interest in our products, it often generates interest in becoming a Beauty Consultant. This is a new and wonderful experience for most women—it's been a long time between compliments. After she has become a Beauty Consultant and has given her first skin care class, her Sales Director *always* seeks something about her to praise. No matter how many mistakes are made during that first class, the new Beauty Consultant is told what she did right. Even though her reaction is usually "What did I do wrong?" we respond, "Let's talk about what you did right." (As Somerset Maugham said, "People ask you for criticism, but they only want praise.") Only after the Beauty Consultant has been praised for her strong points will the Sales Director offer criticism, always sandwiching it in between two thick layers of praise. An even better approach, if the example is of general interest, would be to present it at the next group sales meeting.

Years ago, I knew instinctively that Helen McVoy, one of the original Independent Beauty Consultants who went on to become a National Sales Director, was going to be a tremendous success in our business after I overheard her talking outside my office door with a new Beauty Consultant.

"You had a $35 show? Why, that's wonderful!" she said enthusiastically.

Even then, a $35 show was not so good. I couldn't imagine who she was talking to, so I stepped out of my office to see.

"Mary Kay," Helen said effusively when she saw me, "may I present my new team member. Last night she had a $35 class!" Helen paused for a moment, then lowered her voice. "At her first two shows she didn't sell anything—but last night she sold $35! Isn't that terrific?"

Immediately, I realized that without Helen's praise and encouragement her new team member might never have stayed long enough to do a fourth class. Helen was praising her to success! This kind of praise does wonders to build a person's confidence. By receiving praise for each small achievement, an individual gains confidence to try harder. Thus little successes pave the way to bigger successes.

A small child will stand on wobbly legs, then take a tiny step, only to fall down again. "Oh, isn't that wonderful," a parent will say, making a joyous fuss. "Come on, try it again, honey," the parent coaxes, down on hands and knees, applauding every step. Again and again the child is praised until he actually learns to walk. Without praise from our parents, a lot of us might still be crawling!

The same thing occurs when a baby begins to utter the babbling sounds that precede actual words. A baby says, "Da-da," and the father immediately translates it to mean *Daddy*. *"*Did you hear that!" the proud father shouts excitedly. "She called me Daddy!" He then picks up the baby and hugs and kisses her. "You're such a beautiful girl, and Daddy loves you very much." By receiving praise, the baby is encouraged to talk—and she does!

I believe that in order to be a good leader you must understand the value of *praising people to success*.

Praise is an incredibly effective motivator; unfortunately, many managers are reluctant to employ it. Yet I can't help feeling that they know how much praise means, not only to others, but also to *themselves*. When was the last time you said to somebody at work, "You know, you're really terrific! I admire the fine job you're doing here at the office."

I believe that you should praise people whenever you can; it causes them to respond as a thirsty plant responds to water.

One of our marketing executives demonstrated a clever way to praise employees who had been working long overtime hours. They had been preparing for Seminar—a three-day spectacular convention for the sales force. We had scheduled more than 20,000-plus women to come to Dallas to attend these events. Needless to say, the marketing staff worked months in preparation

and also planned on being on 24-hour call during the convention.
All the employees and their spouses were invited to a unique
dinner-dance called "Hats Off to You." It was a fun party with
more than 100 people, including spouses. The party had a clever
theme, requiring everyone to wear a funny hat. And, while there
were no speeches, throughout the party, the leader kept switching
hats and making the rounds, tipping a different hat to each of his
people. He must have brought dozens of hats to the affair. As he
tipped his hat, he lauded each person for his or her fine performance. "Say, you did a great job," he was overheard telling a
woman in charge of our in-house publication. "I don't know how
you do it, but month after month you come up with a sensational
edition. There's just nothing comparable in American industry,
and this year's pre-promotion of Seminar was just superb. . . . ''

In keeping with this philosophy of recognition, I sincerely
believe that a 40-cent gift given with $100 worth of recognition is
a thousand times more effective than a $100 gift in a dollar box
given with 40 cents of recognition. And I ought to know! I
remember once working day and night for two weeks in a recruiting contest in order to receive a ribbon that said "Miss Dallas."
(It was the only way I was ever going to *be* "Miss Dallas.") I didn't
do it for the ribbon—but for the recognition that it represented.

The power of positive motivation in a goal-oriented structure
such as ours cannot be overstated. This is what inspires our Beauty
Consultants to maximize their true potential. Mary Kay is known
for giving much more than ribbons to those who achieve their
goals. In addition to pink Cadillacs, we award such luxuries as
diamond rings and fabulous trips abroad. A diamond bumblebee
is the ultimate symbol of recognition at Mary Kay. It's the "crown
jewel," and its recipient is recognized as a queen. These special
tributes are presented at Seminar to Super Achievers in sales,
recruiting, and unit performance. On Awards Night the emcee

will announce the winners and present them in a manner similar to the Miss America coronation. Many speeches are given, including congratulatory ones by both my son Richard and myself.

These traditions continue today and have been compared to the most dazzling theatrical productions and awards ceremonies. Around the world, the Mary Kay culture not only fosters a true spirit of praise and recognition, it thrives upon it. At any Mary Kay event, anywhere in the world, you'll find ceremonies praising women toward even greater achievements while they recognize each other's successes. Even a visit to one of the corporate offices is a cause to roll out the red carpet, be applauded by staff, etc.

Applause Is a Powerful Form of Praise

At Seminar, praise and recognition are generously given to the independent sales force in the presence of thousands of their peers, followed by long and loud applause. Newspaper and magazine reporters have described these events at Seminar as the "ultimate" form of praise and, of course, that's exactly what they're intended to be.

Applause is a powerful form of praise. Consider the price actors and actresses are willing to pay for recognition, that one chance in a thousand to "make it to the top." And those who do get an opportunity to perform in front of live audiences must repeat the same lines night after night. Why do they do it? For the applause they receive from an appreciative audience! Although the top stars are well paid, I'm sure it's more than the love of money that motivates them to excellence.

Give as Much Recognition as Possible

Because we recognize the need for people to be praised, we make a concerted effort to give as much recognition as possible. Of course, with an organization as large as ours, not everyone can make a speech at our Seminars, but we do attempt to have many people appear on stage, if only for a few moments, as a reward for their achievements.

How important are these brief stage appearances? Frankly, I think it means more for a woman to be recognized by her peers onstage than to receive an expensive present in the mail that nobody knows about! And once a woman gets a taste of this recognition, she wants to come back next year for more!

Recently I was asked to speak at a top manufacturer's convention. In the evening I was invited to an awards night dinner, and several of their dealers were wearing navy blue sports jackets. I couldn't help noticing how poorly they fit; evidently they hadn't been properly tailored. "Why are those men wearing those jackets?" I asked a company executive.

"Oh, they're our top dealers," I was told.

Throughout the entire banquet, I kept waiting for a speech that would honor those top performers. I thought it was going to be the highlight of the affair. After the dinner there was entertainment by a well-known artist, and then balloons were dropped from the ceiling. "That's a great way to start the recognition part of the banquet," I thought to myself. But that was it. The affair was over, and everybody started to leave.

"What about the awards?" I asked the executive.

"Oh, they've already received their awards—the navy jackets we sent to their rooms."

I was astonished! I couldn't imagine that a company could have sponsored an awards dinner without public recognition of its star performers. At Mary Kay we *never* miss an opportunity to give recognition. I am sure it would have meant far more to those men to have stood up and been applauded than to have received those navy blue jackets!

Another opportunity we use to give praise is in our monthly *Applause*® magazine. Its main purpose, aside from sharing product news, is to give recognition. It's printed in full color, and its circulation is as large as that of many nationally known magazines. I've often said to Beauty Consultants and Sales Directors, "Have you ever noticed how 'wonderful' *Applause*® is when your name's in it, and how it's not quite as interesting when your name is not included?"

Everybody likes to see his or her name in print. But since only a small percentage of people can appear in any one issue of *Applause*®, we encourage every Sales Director to send out her own newsletter. And one of the things we strongly recommend is the inclusion of as many names as possible. That way, in a unit of 100 people, every Beauty Consultant has a good chance for public recognition. We also have a monthly publication for Sales Directors called *Directors Memo*, and there's a monthly publication for our Company employees. While we believe there are four elements in a successful publication—recognition, information, education, and inspiration—our No. 1 purpose is recognition.

In keeping with Mary Kay's belief in the power of praising people to success, several Company publications highlight the extensive recognition programs, including a few with the sole purpose of featuring names and photos of top performers.

I've often had men say to me, "Come on, now, Mary Kay, it may work for you to award ribbons, honor sales leaders onstage before large audiences, and name top achievers in your publications, but this kind of thing doesn't work with men." I just smile when I hear such remarks. Did you ever notice the stars on a six-foot, seven-inch, 275-pound linebacker's helmet? Or the medals on a soldier's uniform? Men are willing to risk bodily injury and even their lives for praise and recognition!

It's interesting to note how some people discount praise. In fact, one of our own male executives frequently says, "Praise is great, but I don't personally need it. My ego doesn't need massaging—save it for somebody else." Frankly, I don't believe it. He, like other people who make that statement, secretly crave praise. I happen to know that this particular executive purrs like a kitten whenever he's praised. Like the rest of us, he loves it.

As a leader, you must recognize that *everyone* needs praise. But it must be given sincerely. You'll find numerous occasions for genuine praise if you'll only look for them. So give. Praise does not thrive in secret! Nor do we.

Independent National Sales Directors Talk about Mary Kay Principles in Action Today

"By praising people to success . . . we awaken sleeping giants that are within people. And huge success happens from there," says former fashion model and part-time math teacher **Cheryl Warfield** of the United States.

"It's so true that in the workplace, people are always told what they are doing wrong, seldom what they do right.

Women blossom like roses when they are encouraged to try and when praised for all their achievements," said **Yvonne Williams** of the United Kingdom, where in 2004, Mary Kay Ash was honored posthumously with the Humanitarian Rose Award at Kensington Palace for the work she inspired through her Foundation and the impact she had on the lives of women throughout the world.

"Praise has caused many women to achieve big things that they didn't even know they could achieve," said **Patricia Hernandez de Bodart** of Mexico who, before succeeding in her Mary Kay business, owned and lost seven businesses due to economic conditions.

"Women come to Mary Kay at different levels of self-confidence and worldly experience. Every single one grows and develops more confidence and courage every time she is sincerely praised," says **Karen Piro** of the United States, who learned of Mary Kay through her friend, currently a nationally prominent network television host.

For **Liliya Shershneva** of Ukraine, learning this chapter, "helped me realize a lot of talent in myself, also to give people confidence in their potential. These principles helped me to love people as they are."

5 The Art of Listening

All through school we're taught to read, write, and speak; yet we're never taught to listen. But while listening may be the most undervalued of all the communication skills, good people managers are likely to listen more than they speak. Perhaps that's why we were given two ears and only one mouth.

Don't Undervalue the Ability to Listen

Some of the most successful leaders are also the best listeners. I remember one in particular. He had been hired by a large corporation to assume the role of sales manager. But he knew absolutely nothing about the specifics of the business. When salespeople would go to him for answers, there wasn't anything he could tell them—because he didn't know anything! Nonetheless, this man *really* knew how to listen. So no matter what they would ask him, he'd answer, "What do *you* think you ought to do?" They'd come up with the solution, he'd agree, and they'd leave satisfied. They thought he was fantastic.

He taught me that valuable listening technique, and I've applied it ever since. One time an Independent Beauty Consultant came to me to discuss her marital problems. She asked my advice as to whether she should divorce her husband. Since I didn't even know the man, and hardly knew her, there was no way I could give her advice. All I did was listen, nod my head, and ask, "What do *you* think you ought to do?" I asked her that several times, and each time she went on to tell me what she thought she should do. The next day I received a beautiful bouquet of flowers with a lovely note thanking me for my terrific advice. Then, about a year later, she wrote to tell me that her marriage was wonderful, and again my advice was credited!

Many of the problems I hear don't require me to offer solutions. I solve most of them by just listening and letting the involved party do the talking. If I listen long enough, the person will generally come up with an adequate solution.

Many years ago, a friend of mine purchased a small manufacturing company at a bargain price. The previous owner said, "I'm glad to get rid of it. My employees have become very militant, and they just don't appreciate all I've done for them over the years. They're going to vote for a union any day now, and I don't want to deal with those union people."

After becoming the owner, my friend conducted an open meeting with his total staff. "I want you all to be happy," he told them. "Tell me what I can do to make that happen." As it turned out, he only had to provide a few minor conveniences: modern bathroom fixtures, larger mirrors in the locker rooms, and vending machines for the recreation area. These were the only things they wanted. As a result, the union was never voted in, and everyone remained content. All they really wanted was someone to listen to them.

Listening is an art. And the first tenet of the skill is paying undivided attention to the other party. When someone enters my office to speak with me, I don't allow anything to distract my attention. If I'm talking to someone in a crowded room, I try to make that person feel as though we're the only ones present. I shut out everything else.

I look directly at the person. Even if a gorilla were to walk into the room, I probably wouldn't notice it. I remember how offended I once was when I was having lunch with my sales manager, and every time a pretty waitress walked by, his eyes would follow her across the room. I felt insulted and kept thinking to myself, "That waitress's legs are more important to him than what I have to say. He's not listening to me. He doesn't care about me!" You've got to pay attention to hear what the other person is saying. Without discipline and concentration, our minds wander.

People also can be distracted by their own petty prejudices. For instance, a person may use profanity or some expression that you don't like. Or perhaps you are irritated by a certain accent. I know Southerners who can't stand a New York accent, and I've met New Yorkers who feel the same way about a Southern drawl. Consequently, they allow something this insignificant to distract from the value of another person's thoughts.

Everyone has seen jokesters who get together to exchange stories. No sooner does one tell a joke than the other person matches him. Neither one listens to the other, because they're both too busy getting their next joke ready. At some point, each of us has failed to listen by restlessly awaiting a turn to speak.

Often people feel uneasy whenever there's a pause in the conversation. They feel compelled to rush in and start talking. Perhaps if they would remain quiet, the other person might clarify or provide additional information. Sometimes it's good for both parties to keep quiet for a few moments to think. A conversation interrupted by silence can be a welcome relief. In fact, nonstop conversation may be an indication that something is seriously wrong.

Many managers make the mistake of creating a boss-employee relationship between themselves and their people—like student to teacher. However, while it is true that a teacher generally stands at the head of the class and does most of the talking, a good teacher also knows how to listen attentively. So does a good manager. To play an authoritarian role with a subordinate establishes a "we-they" adversarial relationship. Effective communication breaks down, and nobody listens.

Sometimes listening by itself may not be enough; some people must be prodded if you are to find out what they're thinking. But a word of caution: Be subtle or you'll come across as being intrusive. Sometimes a thin line separates invasion of privacy from concern and interest. With this in mind, when I sense a problem, I'll ask a question or two, then be quiet and listen for a response. Some time ago, for instance, the work habits of one of my executives, whom I will call "Bill," began to falter. He had always submitted his reports promptly, but for several consecutive weeks he had been arriving at the office late, and at committee meetings he had contributed very little—all of which was quite uncharacteristic of him. One day while he was in my office explaining why a report was late, I decided it was time to have a heart-to-heart talk with him. I stood up from my desk and walked around to pour him a cup of coffee.

"How do you like your coffee?" I asked.

"Black would be fine."

I put his cup on the table in front of the sofa and sat down. He automatically sat down beside me. "Bill," I said, "you're one of our key people, you've been with us for 12 years, and I feel we have become good friends in that time."

"I feel that way, too, Mary Kay," he said in a soft voice.

"I'm concerned about you, Bill. You've always been so consci-entious about your work that we've come to depend upon your contributions. But lately you just haven't been yourself."

He didn't respond, so I stopped talking and took a sip of coffee. He seemed tense, and I offered to pour more coffee for him. "No, that's all right," he answered.

"Is something wrong at home?" I asked.

His face grew red, and after a few moments he nodded his head.

"Is there anything I could do to help?"

He proceeded to tell me how upset he was because his wife's doctor had discovered a tumor on her upper back, and he had wanted to tell me because he knew it was affecting his work. I'm certain it was necessary for him to release his bottled-up feelings, and we must have talked for over an hour. He seemed to feel much better at the end of the conversation, and later his work improved immensely. While I didn't solve his personal problem, it was good for the two of us to talk about it.

Just how far a manager should go in discussing an employee's personal problems is something only the individuals involved can determine. I don't think a manager can work with a person day in and day out and not develop some sort of personal relationship. Of course, you must use discretion at all times and never pry.

If you do ask questions and are subtle about it, you are ex-pressing a genuine interest in what the other person has to say. A doctor who asks you a lot of questions shows that he cares about your health. But a doctor who seems too busy to ask enough questions to diagnose the problem gives you the impression that he really doesn't care and that he's only interested in sending you a bill.

"Tell me, when did you first begin to have this pain in your stomach?" a caring doctor asks. "What were you doing at the time? What did you have to eat just before you noticed it? Have you ever had this before? Does it hurt when I touch you here? How about here?" By asking these questions he not only learns enough to diagnose and treat the problem, but he also demonstrates his concern. At Mary Kay, every person in the Company knows that he or she can bring a problem to my attention at any time.

When we were a very small company, I had a close working relationship with everyone in the organization. In those early days, it was easy to listen regularly to what each person had to say. But now, with so many Independent Beauty Consultants and Company employees, it's physically impossible to always listen in this same way. Nevertheless, each person is just as important as the next and must be heard. Our solution is to impress upon our leaders—through continued training—that listening will always be a top priority.

Your Own Organization Can Be an Invaluable Resource for Ideas

Today our large independent sales force is an invaluable resource that we tap for new ideas. We continually communicate with Independent Beauty Consultants, encouraging them to let us know what's happening from their point of view. Most of the Independent Sales Directors, for example, publish monthly newsletters or updates. Many of their ideas are included in Company publications, always with credit to the originator. The independent sales force constantly gives us feedback. We get hundreds of ideas each month. Although we can't possibly use every one of them, we do express our gratitude to them for sharing their thoughts with us.

THE ART OF LISTENING

The highest position in the independent sales force is that of Independent National Sales Director. Here, too, listening is a priority. The most effective communication mechanism for this group has proved to be a series of smaller advisory groups. At such meetings, we ask these groups to review ideas and offer strategic solutions. Because the Independent National Sales Directors are constantly meeting with Independent Beauty Consultants and Sales Directors, they're able to provide us with valuable information.

Encourage Feedback

It's very important to encourage people to give you feedback, but when you do so, you must abide by three rules:

1. Listen to what they say.
2. Acknowledge all correspondence sent to you.
3. Give proper recognition for all valid suggestions.

By listening to people in the field, we're able to develop products that are the direct result of demands from customers. Consequently, our product development is different from that of cosmetics firms that don't have the advantage of this same kind of feedback. For example, let's say XYZ Cosmetics Company decides that they want to bring out a new eyeliner. After they manufacture it, they give it to their marketing people and say, "Go sell this." Then they advertise it on television, create lavish in-store displays, order saturation mailings and so on. They attempt to create a demand for their product *after* it has been created. We, on the other hand, know what our customers want *before* we create it. The independent sales force tells us: "Our customers want this *size* compact." "Our customers want this shade." "Our customers want the lip brush to do this and this." By listening to what consumers want, our research and development groups introduce products that are consumer-driven. When we add a new water-proof mascara to our product line, for example, it fulfills a demand consumers have expressed to the independent sales force.

"But we aren't set up to listen that closely to our sales representatives," I sometimes hear other company executives explain. If a company with hundreds of thousands of Independent Beauty Consultants can listen, so can every other company—if its leadership really wants to. I knew one national sales manager who called each of his 35 sales representatives at least once a week. Constant communication with the sales force kept him abreast of what was going on in the field. Another sales manager with 40 sales representatives made about 25 random calls to his people each week. "How's it going?" he might say to them in a friendly way. "What can I do for you? If you have any questions, just ask." Both made it perfectly clear they were never too busy to accept a call. At times they were not available, each made a point of returning every call from the salespeople before going to sleep each night.

Although many companies have the opportunity to listen to their sales force, they fail to do so. A very successful life insurance agent once confided to me that his company totally ignores what its field representatives tell the home-office people. "I don't even bother to make suggestions anymore," he told me, "because they don't pay any attention to what I or any other agent has to say. Every time I'd express an idea for a change, our marketing people would say, 'You just stick to selling, and let us worry about what kinds of policies we offer. We have all kinds of experts to design policies—don't even waste your time thinking about it. You do your job and let us do ours.'" Not only was this insurance company shortsighted in not availing itself of some potentially good suggestions, but in the process, it was also hurting the morale of its sales force.

I believe that failing to hear what your people are saying indicates gross negligence in a manager. Fortunately, once you are aware of the importance of listening, it's not a difficult art to practice. Your people will let you know what's happening—if they know they can count on you to listen.

Independent National Sales Directors Talk about
Mary Kay Principles in Action Today

"I discovered that listening was a skill I really needed to learn," says **Norelle Turner-Allen** of Australia, "in order to truly hear what the women on my team were telling me. All of us need this skill of utmost importance to personal growth."

"Listening was my biggest challenge and my greatest learning," says **Anna Ewing**, "because I'm what you might call a mouth! I credit my four brothers with fostering within me a challenging spirit. They reminded me daily that I couldn't do things because I was a girl. It became my duty to run faster, climb higher, and throw a ball farther," says the Texan who started her Mary Kay business two years after the founding.

"This awesome Company was built on our customers' falling in love with Mary Kay® products and on our listening to their needs. When they are pampered, learn how to use the product, and develop a trusting relationship, then customer loyalty and repeat business will come," says **Judy Kawiecki** of the United States. A marketing researcher by profession, her Mary Kay business flexibility allowed Judy to be the primary caregiver when her husband was diagnosed with a heart condition; in caring for his sister with cerebral palsy; and during her own mother's terminal illness. "I shudder to think what would have happened with my former corporate position during all this," she says today.

6 Sandwich Every Bit of Criticism between Two Heavy Layers of Praise

I don't think it's ever appropriate for a manager to criticize an individual. Not that criticism should never be given; there are times when a manager *must* communicate dissatisfaction. But the criticism should be directed at *what's* wrong—not at *who's* wrong!

It's Pollyannaish not to express your feelings when someone has done something wrong. But it must be done tactfully; otherwise, your criticism will be destructive. I feel that a manager should be able to tell someone when something is wrong without bruising an ego in the process.

When someone enters my office, it is important that I create an atmosphere conducive to communication. And I find that this is most easily accomplished when I remove the physical barrier of an office desk. That desk represents authority. It tells the person sitting on the other side that I am in a position to tell him what he *must* do. I'd rather come across as a friend and co-worker—not as "the boss." And so we sit on a comfortable sofa and discuss our business in a more relaxed environment.

I believe in the power of touch. It's something that comes naturally to me, so I feel comfortable doing it. It puts the other person at ease. You may sense that a handshake is best with one individual; with another, a pat on the back; and with somebody else, a big hug. We've all heard stories about doctors who utilize good bedside manners and who "hold a patient's hand." Well, similarly, for a manager there are times when you should display a good "couchside" manner. So go ahead, reach out and *touch* someone—it's good people management.

Be Tender and Tough

I believe that it's okay for a manager to develop a relationship with his or her employees. In fact, I don't think it's natural for people who continually work together to always be "on ceremony," always maintaining a formal employer-employee relationship. I don't think this kind of atmosphere is conducive to maximum productivity. For generations it has been preached to us that "familiarity breeds contempt." The military is a good example, with its strict codes that prohibit officers from fraternizing with enlisted personnel. Such attitudes often spill over into the workplace, and frankly, I do not personally believe they're appropriate. Drawing a line between you and the other person inhibits good working relationships, particularly whenever it's necessary to have a heart-to-heart talk with him or her.

At the same time, managers must be strong and speak straightforwardly. If someone's work is unsatisfactory, you can't skirt the issue—you must communicate your feelings. This calls for being simultaneously tender and tough. In other words, you've got to maintain your manager role, but you must also have empathy. A fine line exists between being too buddy-buddy and compromising your supervisory status. In a way, it can be compared to a big brother/big sister relationship—a role that can combine love and compassion, but also can resort to disciplinary action if necessary. In fact, to many of our people, my own image is motherly. They regard me as somebody who cares so much about them that they want to confide in me. Many times I've heard, "Mary Kay, my mother passed away several years ago, and I look upon you as my mother now." I am very honored when I hear this.

Never Give Criticism without Praise

Never giving criticism *without* praise is a strict rule for me. No matter what you are criticizing, you must find something good to say—both *before* and *after*. This is what's known as the "sandwich technique."

Criticize the act, not the person. And try to praise in the beginning and then again *after* discussing the problem. Also strive to end on a friendly note. By handling the problem this way, you don't subject people to harsh criticism or provoke anger.

I've seen some managers operate on the theory that when they're angry about something, they should criticize the person and let him know exactly how they feel about his actions. This school of thought proposes that you should express your emotions—let the other person have it, no punches pulled. After the manager has had sufficient time to vent his anger, he's supposed to end it with a word of praise, and theoretically, everything will be okay again. While some management consultants advocate this technique, I cannot condone it. A person who is treated in this manner will be so shaken by the harsh criticism that he'll never hear the praise, which is so obviously thrown in as an afterthought. This kind of criticism is destructive—not constructive.

I believe that all of us have fragile egos and that we respond much better to praise than to criticism. A woman, for instance, can buy a new dress that she falls in love with; but let her hear one bit of criticism, and she'll never wear it again. I remember buying a pink organdy dress and getting ready to attend a dinner party. I thought it was beautiful, and I was pleased at how good I looked in it. My daughter, Marylyn, had a different opinion however.

"Mother, you're not going to wear that dress, are you?"

"Why, yes," I replied somewhat taken aback.

"But, Mother, you look like a cow in it," she told me.

I don't have to tell you that I took the dress off. Not only didn't I wear it that night; I never wore it again. But tell me, "Gee, you look absolutely beautiful in blue. It brings out the color of your eyes," and I'll have a difficult time not wearing a blue dress the next day.

It's possible that some women have a more difficult time handling criticism than do men. Some just take criticism more personally. In my day and age, a woman's cultural background was different from a man's. Men, for instance, received more criticism as youngsters participating in team sports than did women. A coach would shout at a boy for what he did or didn't do or possibly blame him for causing the team to lose. But once the game was over, the boy was taught to accept defeat gracefully and do his best to win the next time. Until recent times, few women were exposed to that environment; consequently, they were apt to take criticism and defeat a little more personally. By and large, women in my day lived more sheltered lives as young persons and did not have to face the harsh criticism to which young boys were often subjected. For this reason, I've always advised handling criticism with a very gentle touch.

Never Give Criticism in Front of Others

It's inexcusable for a manager to chastise someone in the presence of others. Yet I've seen managers who, while addressing a group, will single out one person for criticism. I can't imagine anything more demoralizing.

It's not only self-defeating to criticize someone in front of others, it's also downright cruel. A plant manager, for instance, should never berate a foreman in front of assembly-line workers. Imagine the repercussions if a manager spot-checking quality control were to shout at a foreman, "Look what you're allowing your people to put through, Joe. You know the company can't accept this kind of inferior quality. You're running a third-rate operation here. Just keep it up and you won't be around here very long."

Not only does such action create bitter resentment, but everyone present becomes embarrassed and insecure. A "Will I be next?" atmosphere is created, everyone feels threatened, and productivity suffers. In this case, the workers may have begun to question the ability of their foreman, thereby reducing *his* effectiveness as a manager. Moreover, the foreman's self-esteem would have been badly bruised, making him unsure and hesitant. Although the poor quality of work may have been a very real problem, the manager's clumsy handling of the matter could have only aggravated the situation. Rather than publicly attacking the foreman, the manager should have privately discussed the issue. I think this would have enhanced the probability of solving a legitimate production problem, and it would have preserved the morale of both the foreman and his workers. All parties, including the company, would have then profited.

There is a technique I use when I'm addressing a group of people that permits me to offer effective criticism without hurting anyone. Once I conducted a sales meeting with a group of Independent Beauty Consultants, and there was a particular woman whose beauty kit was simply dirty. She was a new Beauty Consultant, and I felt that her messy kit was causing her to lose sales. However, this woman lacked self-esteem, and I felt that if I confronted her with my complaint on a one-on-one basis, it might crush her. Instead I decided to get my message across in a more subtle way—I'd tell her during my sales meeting, which was titled "Cleanliness Is Next to Godliness." She wouldn't know it, but the message was tailor-made for her benefit. While the others would also learn from my presentation, this woman would accept my criticism without even knowing I was directing it almost exclusively at her!

Throughout the meeting, I spoke about how important it is for every Independent Beauty Consultant to project professionalism. "What would *you* think if you were attending a beauty show and the Beauty Consultant's kit was dirty?" I asked the group. "We're in the beauty business, and we must always project an image of cleanliness," I continued. As I spoke I never once looked at the woman for whose benefit the entire message was intended. I didn't have to. She knew perfectly well that she was guilty, and she must have been thinking, "My kit is a mess." Have you ever listened to a Sunday sermon in church and been positive that the minister was aiming his message directly at you? "How did he know?" you would say to yourself. At the same time you would think, "No it can't be." The minister's point got through to you perfectly but without causing any embarrassment.

A good people manager will never put someone down; not only is it nonproductive, it's counterproductive. You must remember that your job is to play the role of problem solver; by taking this approach instead of criticizing people, you'll accomplish considerably more.

I'm reminded of a situation that existed with one of our Independent Beauty Consultants. (For illustration, I'll call her Margaret.) At one time Margaret had been an excellent sales person, but then something happened. Her enthusiasm waned, she lost interest in her business, and finally she simply stopped attending sales meetings. This is a problem faced by many managers: how to rekindle the spark that you know a worker once possessed.

I called Margaret's Independent Sales Director and asked if she could give Margaret an important role in the next unit sales meeting. Her greatest problem seemed to be in the area of bookings, and so I suggested Margaret be asked to address the group on this topic.

"Perhaps she could instruct the others on the best way to initiate and follow through with bookings," I said.

On the evening of the unit sales meeting, we were overwhelmed. In researching her "problem area," Margaret had reviewed and reanalyzed all the principles and techniques she had once used so successfully. She inspired everyone in the unit, but more importantly, she convinced herself that she, too, could be successful again.

When you approach problems in this fashion, first by placing yourself in the other person's shoes and then by working together to solve the problem, you don't come across as being a harsh critic. You become a helpful friend. The person feels she has an ally who's helping solve the problem. When you identify this as your position, your new "friend" will not only be grateful, but she'll also do her best not to let you down.

Independent National Sales Directors Talk about
Mary Kay Principles in Action Today

"For some reason, the world usually works to correct, shape, and improve us by telling us what we're doing wrong and then how to do it better. All with good intentions, but it's much more effective to find what people are doing right and sandwich criticism in the middle of praise. This is true whether you are dealing in business or with your own children or family. It works in all relationships," says **Carol Stoops**, the mother of three who's married to Bob Stoops, one of the most successful U.S. college football coaches.

"Only with positive feedback can energy grow," says **Maria Brausam-Drogosch** of Germany, a mother and homemaker who was looking for fulfillment and professional recognition when she found the Mary Kay opportunity.

"There's a wonderful continuation of this practice among Mary Kay leaders. I know for a fact that my Senior Sales Director poured belief into me in the early days of my business. She had to look hard, but she caught me doing 'something' right; and she built me up with her praise. As I grew my team, I passed that on and took ownership of it to the degree that it became as much a habit as tooth brushing," says **Pamela Waldrop Shaw** of the United States, a former high school English teacher.

7 Be a Follow-Through Person

I once heard someone say, "Ideas are a dime a dozen, but the men and women who implement them are priceless." How true! The world is full of idea people who are motivated by the best of intentions but who never seem to perform. Such people make poor leaders.

Nothing Great Is Ever Accomplished without Follow-Through

Earlier I discussed the importance of listening to your people. But an equally important step is to then show them that you have acted upon their concerns. When we are presented with a problem or a suggestion from any level within the independent sales force, we follow a set procedure:

- Listen
- Involve others to help formulate a solution
- Follow through

We once had a "We Heard You" program that helped us listen very carefully to what people had to say, but more importantly, indicated action in response to what we heard. This kind of follow through consists of:

1. Analyzing the technical or procedural applicability of a possible solution,

2. Testing the solution with target groups,

3. Taking these results to the general body of associates (in our case, Independent Beauty Consultants and Sales Directors),

4. Enlisting the support of all,

5. Implementing change.

I can illustrate this point with a simple example. Once, our top executives were meeting for two days with National Sales Directors to discuss challenges in team-building. Since they were expressing concerns from the field, this became the highest priority. Our marketing people went to work digesting every suggestion the National Sales Directors had offered. Brainstorming sessions may have lasted all day in search of the right solution to a specific problem. The ideas that evolved from those meetings were condensed into a 12-page report. Then 10 representatives selected by the other National Sales Directors came in for a conference. We felt it would be more expedient to work with an advisory committee rather than a larger group. The next step was to sit down with them and say, "Here's what we think about the challenges, and we want to know what you think." They were able to see how hard we had worked to come up with suggested solutions, and that only with their concurrence would any change be considered.

This most clearly illustrates a primary element in the philosophy of Mary Kay: "People will support that which they help to create." When you *dictate* even the most thoughtful and logical concept to a person, this idea is still a command. When you ask her to contribute to its inception, that very same idea becomes a "personal crusade." She suddenly feels a responsibility to ensure its success.

The advisory committee reacted to our suggested solutions and offered more feedback. They liked some of our ideas—but certainly not everything. We returned to the conference table and spent many more hours making revisions to comply with the advisory committee's suggestions. Once again we presented our ideas to the committee. After further modifications, we finally came up with something that was agreeable to the entire group.

Having secured the Independent National Sales Directors' support, the next phase of our follow-through was enlisting support from the Sales Directors. Each year we conduct Leadership Conference in a different city, and the next conference had already been scheduled. Realizing that it's natural for people to resist change, we immediately began to prepare our presentations of the new ideas to Sales Directors and to solidify the endorsements of the National Sales Directors.

During each conference we experienced very little resistance because we had clearly demonstrated that:

1. The original ideas had come from the "grass roots" of the organization,
2. We had done our homework by carefully thinking through all phases of the solution,
3. We had involved target groups (National Sales Directors) and had engendered their support.

But the procedure also succeeded because of a fourth element already firmly accepted. This was our "in-place" communication mechanism of listening, involving others to help formulate solutions, and following through. Every one of hundreds of thousands of Beauty Consultants knows that she can present an idea that will be fairly judged in an open forum, refined and perhaps restructured by others, and then possibly implemented by all. Each idea has an equal chance of rising or falling by the weight of its own merits. I think this is significantly different from those organizations in which you must hold a high position before your ideas will be translated into action.

The Best Kind of Follow-Through Is Immediate

Managers can also fail when follow-through takes too much time. An automobile salesman once told me how he and 14 other salespeople had gone to their dealer and sales manager to express major grievances. "We had some bitter complaints about the commission schedules, the fringe benefits, and the long evening hours," he told me, "so one Sunday afternoon we all met for four hours at the boss's home to review these problems. Our dealer and the sales manager listened attentively and were in full agreement that our compensation plan was obsolete and noncompetitive with other dealerships in town. We put in a lot of hours that day, but we all went home very happy, because we felt that we finally got through to management the fact that our problems were very real. We thought the meeting had been a huge success."

"That's wonderful," I said. "You've got to give them credit for being good listeners."

"Oh, they listened magnificently," he said, "but that's all they did. They never followed through on a single thing. Weeks and then months went by without a single word from them on what changes would result from the meeting. Every time we'd bring up the subject, they'd have some sort of excuse. 'This is a bad time to discuss it,' or 'Don't worry, we'll get to it—but don't expect changes to happen overnight.'"

"It must have been very demoralizing," I commented.

"As bad as morale had been, it got even worse, Mary Kay. Three months after the meeting, four of our salesmen had quit, and sales totals by those of us who remained had dropped considerably."

Eventually these car salesmen did get what they were after. But the changes weren't appreciated because of the length of time required to implement them, and the goodwill that could have been gained by immediate follow-through was lost.

Trust is also an important element of follow-through. A branch manager of a department store told me about an inexcusable act committed by his district manger. "My buyers were very upset over the company's policy regarding travel allowances for buying trips," the branch manager told me. "I, in turn, explained these complaints to my district manager during one of his trips to Dallas. The district manager assured me that he would immediately see to it that certain changes were made to satisfy what he considered to be both realistic and justifiable. 'I'll call you at the end of the week to let you know that the home office has given its approval,' he told me."

The hitch, however, was that the branch manager told his buyers to be expecting those changes guaranteed by the district manager.

"I wanted to let them know immediately because they were all getting ready to leave on a major buying trip to New York the following Monday morning, and I wanted to cheer them up. But at the end of the week, my district manager called me and said, 'I'm sorry, but there are some complications. I won't be able to help your buyers this trip. But don't worry, we'll get them what they want in time for their next trip.' To make a long story short, Mary Kay, the home office turned down the change that he had 'guaranteed.' It upset my buyers so much that I lost two of them to another local department store."

Never Make a Promise You Can't Keep

While this district manager was probably acting in good faith, in his overzealous effort to please the branch manger he showed poor judgment. A manager should never make a promise that something will be done unless he is absolutely certain that it *will* be done! A broken promise is devastating for those who have been disappointed, and there is no excuse for it in management. Furthermore, a manager should never make a commitment unless he has the complete authority to do so. In the preceding case, the district manager would have been wise to say, "I've heard all of the grievances, and I will take them back to the home office and get back to you shortly. I'll see what I can do." If he felt strongly that certain changes should be made, he might have added, "I can't give you any guarantees, but I do want you to know that I'm in agreement with you—and that I'll do my best to argue your cause with my superiors." By saying this, he would have demonstrated his support and also offered what he felt was needed—on-the-spot encouragement. Then, had he failed (as in this illustration), his expression of hope would not have backfired. I think it's best to use the utmost caution—false hope is destructive.

Follow-Through Requires Discipline and Planning

Correspondence is an area in which people often fail to follow through. Most of us don't like to write, and we naturally tend to put off those things we don't like to do. But people do become irritated, and justly so, when they receive no response to their letters. In fact, most people take it as a personal insult. So if you're looking for a good way *not* to influence people—leave your mail unanswered. (The same goes for unreturned telephone calls.)

I always answer my mail. If the subject falls in another person's area of expertise, I make certain that it's appropriately forwarded. However, since it was addressed to me, I'm the one the sender expects to reply. So when I send it to a third party, it is still my responsibility to make certain that it's answered. In order to ensure that the matter gets a quick response, I attach an action tab requesting that a copy of the reply be sent to me. Unfortunately, we have a few managers who don't follow up on their letters as well as they should, so each Friday I review my files, and if I haven't received my copy, I keep asking until I get it. That's follow-through.

There are many tasks that all of us are required to do but prefer to avoid. Writing letters is only one example. This trait reminds me of a story I once heard about Ivy Lee, a renowned efficiency expert, who called on Charles Schwab, former president of Bethlehem Steel. "If I could increase your people's efficiency—and your sales—by spending just 15 minutes with each of your executives, would you hire me to do the job?" Lee asked Schwab.

"How much would it cost me?" Schwab inquired.

"Nothing—unless it works. In three months you can decide and send me a check for whatever you feel it was worth."

The industrialist nodded his head in agreement.

Then Lee proceeded to conduct individual meetings with all the Bethlehem Steel executives in which he asked each person to make a promise. For the next 90 days, before leaving his office at the end of the day, the executive was instructed to make a list of the six most important things he had to do the next day and number them in order of their importance. The executive was told to scratch off each item after finishing it and go on to the next number. If something wasn't done, it was added to the following day's list. At the end of the 90-day period, the increase in efficiency and sales had pleased Schwab so much that he sent Lee a check for $35,000. Lee had taught them follow-through—and that was a quality for which

Schwab was willing to pay a lot of money. I was so impressed by the story's message that, ever since, I've made up my own daily list. And it's worked wonderfully for me.

My list keeps me on track, and I give it all the credit when people tell me how well I follow up. I write down everything that requires follow-through, and once on paper, it becomes a tangible commitment that I *must* attend to. It also disciplines me to do those things I'd rather not do—the kinds of things that most people tend to put off and never get around to doing. I've taught independent sales force members to do the same thing, and I always tell them: Don't trust it to memory. If you don't write it down, you'll never get around to doing even the most well-intended task. We also provide a Six Most Important Things notepad—and the people who use it realize measurable improvement in their time-management efficiency.

Increasing my workday also provides me with more time to be a better follow-through person. Some time ago I reasoned that since there are only 24 hours in a day, the only way I could get more mileage out of those hours was by rising at 5 A.M. each morning. With no phone calls or other interruptions, those early morning hours are very productive. Word got around throughout the sales force about what time I get up, and that started the Mary Kay Five O'Clock Club. When I ask an audience of new Independent Sales Directors how many are willing to join the club, it's amazing how many hands go up. "Okay, that's great," I say. "Now, one of these mornings I'm going to give you a call at 5:30, and I'm going to ask you to read your Six Most Important Things list. How many of you *still* want to be in the Five O'Clock Club?" Surprisingly, they still raise their hands—and I have been known to follow through on that call!

From the very beginning we teach each of the Independent Beauty Consultants the importance of follow-through. She's taught to regularly call her customers and say, "Tell me how you are doing. How is the product working for you?" We're probably the only cosmetics company in the world whose representatives routinely follow up with a customer after she has made a purchase. The Beauty Consultant doesn't do it to get more business, because the customer hasn't yet had time to use up what she initially bought. She follows up like this because if there is a problem, she wants to nip it in the bud. Suppose, for instance, a customer's facial skin was still too dry. The Beauty Consultant would substitute another skin-care formula and maintain contact to ensure the customer is completely satisfied.

Two months after that contact, the new Beauty Consultant is encouraged to follow up again with the customer. To make this easier, we provide her with a filing tab system that reminds her when the customer is ready to reorder. Success in our business depends on customer satisfaction—a one-time order is not what we're after. Every Beauty Consultant is taught to give outstanding service, which is by far the best way to ensure repeat business. Those Beauty Consultants who apply this special brand of follow-through with their customers are the ones who eventually become the best Sales Directors. After all my years of experience in selling, I would conclude that servicing the customer is the common denominator shared by all great salespeople and sales managers.

Advanced technology helps Mary Kay Inc. continue to provide cutting-edge support for each independent sales force member with access to an Internet connection. An Independent Beauty Consultant can log in to Company-managed database systems that provide individualized business profiles, including sales data and goal-tracking information as well as recognition. Other functions help her organize customer contact timetables and product

preferences. Additionally, everything from late-breaking
Company news to educational material is available online.
At the Company Web site, www.marykay.com, the public
can access not only Mary Kay® products and programs,
but more on the philosophies.

Independent National Sales Director Dalene White (who was
the first Mary Kay Independent Beauty Consultant), once
conducted an interesting experiment. She called the New York
Stock Exchange to ask the price of 1 ounce of gold. Next she
weighed out 1 ounce of "pink tickets" (carbons of her customers'
sales receipts) and began calling these customers for reorders. At
the end of the day the *profit* from those sales was greater than the
value of an ounce of gold! In calling her customers she had
effectively proved the wisdom of follow-through.

Outstanding leaders extend the same degree of follow-through to
their sales teams by asking, "Tell me about your day." After listening
carefully, he/she might add, "If you don't mind, I'd like to make a
few calls with you tomorrow and see if I can offer some assistance."

Do Your Homework

This chapter contains several examples of following through with
projects. All rely upon a personal technique that can be called
"doing your homework." Whether following through with major
changes within a company, such as when we responded to the
National Sales Directors and reevaluated current practices, *or*
whether following through on a single customer's preference for a
lip color, the task is much simpler if you learn how to research,
organize, prepare, and practice.

If you have ever faced an audience, then you understand the importance of doing your homework. A well-delivered speech requires researching your subject, organizing and preparing your material, and practicing your delivery. Very few people can give an outstanding impromptu speech, although a good speaker often leaves you with the impression that she has. But timing and delivery must be rehearsed again and again until the actual speech comes across as spontaneous. I, for instance, like many other speakers, have delivered my share of spur-of-the-moment speeches, and people have expressed surprise that I was able to speak for more than an hour without notes. "You were wonderful, Mary Kay," I'm told. "You have such a talent for speaking without any preparation."

For the record, however, those are the speeches that I'm *best* prepared to give. There are many subjects that over the years I have learned so well, I don't need additional preparation to speak about them. But let me emphasize that it took *years* to get to the point where I am armed with enough experiences to tell my story extemporaneously. Even today, if I agree to give a speech on a topic outside my area of expertise, I'll spend hours preparing for it.

The most important weekly events within the independent sales force are the Sales Director unit meetings. Monday seems the best time for these meetings, because it marks a "new beginning." To some people, this is the end of a carefree weekend and referred to as "blue Monday." In addition to being informative, these meetings provide both inspiration and motivation. Even if the last week's sales were poor, here's a new week to start fresh. We often say, "If you had a bad week, *you* need the meeting; if you had a good week, the meeting needs *you*!" When a Beauty Consultant leaves a sales meeting full of enthusiasm, she has an entire week to let that enthusiasm work for her.

It's essential for a Sales Director to conduct an effective meeting, but it doesn't just happen; she has to do her homework. If she doesn't, the women in her unit won't get anything useful out of the meeting, and they will soon stop attending. They won't get dressed and go each week if nothing is accomplished. If attendance falls off, the production of her unit will take a nose dive, so we can generally tell which Sales Directors aren't conducting stimulating meetings. At any given time, we have many new Sales Directors who have not yet become adept at running an effective meeting. Knowing how important these meetings are, we help each Sales Director do her homework. Detailed planning material is made available for this purpose.

We want Beauty Consultants to be experts on both product and skin care techniques. While it's important for all salespeople to know their business thoroughly, we feel particularly strong about this point, because these Beauty Consultants conduct skin care classes. As "instructors" they have an added responsibility over and above the average salesperson. In order to be an expert, each of them must pay the price demanded and *do her homework*. It's presumptuous for any salesperson to walk into a prospect's office without being adequately prepared to give a complete and informative presentation. Yet I've witnessed many who were so inept that they couldn't answer even the most basic questions about their product. When this happens, a salesperson is not only wasting the other person's time, but insulting him as well. Naturally there are times when a legitimate question is asked that a salesperson cannot answer on the spot. For example, if a new Beauty Consultant is asked, "What's the pH factor of this cleansing cream?" She might reply, "You know, nobody has ever asked me that before, but I'll find out and get back to you with the answer."

Of course, a salesperson's job involves other forms of homework in addition to product knowledge and selling techniques. There are many behind-the-scenes details that must be addressed. Being well-organized is vital if you are to maximize the use of

your time. Back in the 1960s, my late husband, Mel, was a manufacturer's representative, and he was a real pro at researching his
customers. He even went so far as to keep a little black book with
such information as a customer's special interests, including
hobbies and sports; his spouse's name; his children's names; and
the receptionist's and secretary's names. He even knew what kinds
of flowers and candies to send a secretary. These, too, were jotted
down in his little black book! He'd travel to Cleveland, for
instance, and call on 10 different accounts knowing all kinds of
personal data about each of them. Mel never had a problem getting
in, because he was so well-liked by everyone. He did his
homework, and it paid off.

As a People Manager, You, Too, Have a Constant Selling Job

Although you might not sell an actual product or service, you
must sell your ideas in order to gain the support of others with
whom you work. With this is mind, you must prepare in advance
for every meeting. Doing your homework for a meeting with a
single person is just as important as it is for a staff meeting, a
board of directors' meeting, or a convention with an audience of
thousands. It would be foolhardy to do otherwise. As an example
of how we should prepare for a meeting, let me elaborate about
that National Sales Directors' meeting discussed at the beginning
of the chapter. As you will recall, there was one major topic up
for discussion. Before the meeting, we came up with every con-
ceivable fact that was pertinent. We could only anticipate the
comments and questions the National Sales Directors might
present to us, but whatever they were, we wanted to be fully prepared. My son Richard presided, and he had all kinds of information at his fingertips. He was able to cite how current economic
factors relating to inflation, unemployment, and disposable

income might affect our efforts. He also rattled off statistics to draw a parallel between the present and past years, based on like and unlike periods. He discussed certain current trends in the direct-sales industry and how they might possibly affect independent sales force efforts. There wasn't a question on the subject that Richard hadn't researched, and everyone was impressed by the extent of his preparation.

While such preparation obviously makes for a well-run meeting, it also accomplishes something else: It generates confidence in the leadership ability. People are annoyed when someone leading a meeting is unprepared. They're likely to think he's completely disorganized or simply doesn't care! In either case, those attitudes are self-defeating. Good people managers convey the impression that they are both efficient and caring.

There's a great deal of truth in the adage, "If you want something done, give it to a busy person." Somehow they always seem to have the capacity to take on one more project. I know top executives in Dallas who are repeatedly called upon by the community to support various charitable and civic causes. No matter how busy they are with their careers and extracurricular activities, they somehow muster up additional time and energy—and they never fail to do a superior job. They are greatly admired by the community because they have earned the reputations of being people who follow through on their commitments.

I also think it takes a great deal of time-management skill for a woman to wear the many hats of wife, mother, homemaker, chauffeur, cook, psychologist, et cetera *and* put in long hours of volunteer work for the community. A woman who can accomplish so much must practice follow-through. And although her résumé may show that she has never worked for remuneration, in my book her background qualifies her for many positions in the business world. Among the Mary Kay independent sales force, we see many women who enter the job market for the first time.

Over the years, I have observed that those who are blessed with the most talent don't necessarily outperform everyone else. It's the people with follow-through who excel. This is true in all walks of life—in business, sports and the arts. I see it constantly in the sales field. And you can see it happen with young people in school. The top students in a class aren't necessarily those with the highest IQs; they're the ones with the best study habits. They consistently follow through every day with their assignments. The real achievers in this world are those who follow through in all things, big and small.

Independent National Sales Directors Talk about Mary Kay Principles in Action Today

When her economics degree landed her in New York working for an agency Mary Kay contracts with, she gained unique insight into the Company. She decided later to begin a Mary Kay business. "When I moved to Mexico from the U.S., I knew that giving my skin care classes—even in another language—would be an inspiration for my team. The lesson is that everything is possible when you follow through on your commitment. Our business success and our mission are strictly related to our capacity to connect with people," says Independent National Sales Director **Francine A. Bracco de Bucio** of Mexico.

"We must each continue to be a follow-through person of our word. We check with our clients to service them, and we work continuously with our teams to educate and guide. Both groups must know that we can be counted on for these things," says **Nancy Moser** of the United States, a dental hygienist who was pursuing a master's in speech pathology the day she walked out of the dentist's office never to return. "I was drawn to this Company because of its positive, action-oriented, problem-solving attitude."

"By helping others set goals and following through to assist them in making a plan to achieve those goals, we are being the good leaders and mentors Mary Kay intended," says Canada's **Donna Weir**, a former cowgirl who initially was attracted to a Mary Kay business because she wanted to earn an extra $50 a week. "I believe in following through with praise each step of the way. One of the best lessons I learned from Mary Kay early in my career was that I cannot ask my team members to do anything I'm not prepared to do first myself."

8 Enthusiasm . . . Moves Mountains!

Nothing great is ever achieved without enthusiasm. We believe this so much that we even have a Company song entitled "I've Got That Mary Kay Enthusiasm."

We have many of our own songs, and they're sung at sales force events ranging from small weekly meetings to our annual Seminars. The independent sales force enjoys this activity, and I believe the singing creates a wonderful esprit de corps. Yet outsiders, especially men, often criticize our singing as being "strictly for women." I disagree. Singing unites people. It's like those "rah-rah-rah for our team" cheers. If someone is depressed, singing will often bring her out of it. Perhaps that's why church services begin with hymns. I can remember many Sunday mornings when I drove my three children to church, and by the time we arrived, their antics in the backseat had made me feel less than reverent. After a few hymns, however, I felt renewed and was able to enter into the mood of the service.

A Good Leader Arouses Enthusiasm

It's unusual for a company to have songs, and over the years, we've receive a lot of publicity about this point. In fact, for many people, Mary Kay Inc. is directly associated with enthusiasm. We're proud of this identity, because enthusiasm is a valuable quality for anyone, regardless of the kind of work he or she does. Many talented individuals fail for lack of enthusiasm, and many leaders fail for lack of support from their people. I truly believe that a mediocre idea that generates enthusiasm will go further than a great idea that inspires no one. For this reason, leaders must be able to arouse enthusiasm in their people. And in order to accomplish this, they themselves must first be enthusiastic.

Of course, nobody can be "up" all the time, and contrary to what many people may think about me, I'm not always up either. I just don't let anyone know when I'm not! Early in my sales career, about a year after my divorce from my first husband, I had considered myself a failure as a woman, as a wife, and as a person. My marriage had failed, and my poor emotional state had caused physical symptoms that several doctors had diagnosed as rheumatoid arthritis. One specialist said my condition was progressing so rapidly that in a matter of months I'd be hopelessly disabled. With three young children to support, that was a horrendous thought!

At the time, I was working for a company that sold home products through a party plan. My livelihood depended on my giving three parties a day, averaging $25 to $40 each. If I were to survive, I had to leave my personal problems at home. So I was determined to always "go in there with a smile," no matter how I felt. In retrospect, I think my physical symptoms were induced by extreme emotional stress, because the more successful I was in selling, the more my health improved. At first the doctors were skeptical—insisting that my improved health was simply a case of remission and that the arthritis would eventually disable me. But as my sales increased, so did my health, and I've never had any symptoms of arthritis since.

Like everyone else, I still have days when I don't feel like working. That's when I have to struggle a bit to muster up my usual enthusiasm. A very successful man once told me, "Mary Kay, if I only went to work on the days I felt like it, I'd never go to work!" I'm certain that if we were honest, we would all admit to having those days when we simply have to give ourselves a little pep talk. So you do it. It's easy to be enthusiastic when everything is going smoothly. But the real test of one's mettle is to maintain enthusiasm under adverse conditions. We often tell our Independent Beauty Consultants, "You've got to fake it until you make it!" That is, act enthusiastic and you will become enthusiastic.

Some time ago we invited a prominent speaker to give a motivational speech at one of our Seminars. His plane was delayed, and he was still on his way from the airport when it became his turn to speak. As emcee, I kept improvising until I received a signal from offstage that he had arrived. As I began my introduction, I glanced over and noticed him pacing back and forth behind the curtains, then jumping up and down and beating on his chest. "What kind of person am I introducing?" I asked myself.

When I finished the introduction, he came running out onstage and gave a fantastic speech to an enthusiastic audience. As I sat next to him at lunch, I said, "You made a nervous wreck out of me. Why did you jump up and down and beat on your chest while I was introducing you?"

"Well, I'm sure you know how it is, Mary Kay," he explained. "My job is motivation, but some days I just don't feel up to par, and it's hard to get out there and give a motivational speech. Today was one of those days. I've had an exhausting morning with the flight delay, and by the time I arrived here I felt drained. Yet I knew you were expecting an enthusiastic, lively speaker, and I didn't want to rain on your parade. So I had to churn up my blood with some exercise and chest-beating." As a manager, you'll have days when you're frustrated or depressed and must still inspire others. Everybody has those days. When you're not feeling up to par, you've simply got to work harder because your attitude can affect the enthusiasm of your people. I can recall many instances when I've been totally exasperated, and still I've *had* to "put my best foot forward." Of all those times when I've heaved a sigh and literally pushed up the corners of my mouth, none was more dramatic than when I appeared on the television program *60 Minutes*.

I'm comfortable speaking before large groups, but being interviewed in my home before an audience of 43 million viewers was daunting!

Our shooting schedule had to be flexible since the program's producers never knew when a late-breaking news story would take precedence. I knew they were coming, but I didn't know exactly when. And so the morning before we had been told they were definitely on their way, I whisked through the house straightening pillows, repositioning plants, and trying to spot even the slightest flaw that could pop out when *60 Minutes* was shown across America.

My home is furnished in soft spring colors, and I must admit that on this day, as the sun filled the room, everything looked perfect. Suddenly I was jarred back to reality—the vacuum cleaner had chipped pale yellow enamel off the baseboard. How could I have missed anything so obvious? Actually they were small chips, but in my anxiety they looked like moon craters. I rushed to the cupboard for a quart of matching enamel, made a swing through the bathroom for a lip brush, got down on my hands and knees, and proceeded to touch up the woodwork. Wanting to help, my husband, Mel, decided to vacuum any dust that could settle in the wet paint. He was using the central vac-uum system—the kind with a very long hose. Surely you know what happened next! That quart of paint spilled all over the middle of the living room carpet. The word "mess" does not adequately describe the scene! I had some turpentine for cleaning the brush, so I poured it in the center of the huge yellow glob. It looked better, but certainly not good enough to be on television! If there was ever a moment when I wanted to just sit down and cry in utter frustration, this was it. It was a holiday and no hardware stores would be open, but turning to Mel and in the calmest voice I could muster, I said, "Surely there's a store open somewhere. Please find us more turpentine."

In 10 minutes he was back with a gallon of paint thinner. I forgot all about my new manicure, of course, and set to work using every towel in the house to sop paint and turpentine out of the carpet.

The next morning when the television crew arrived, I pushed up the corners of my mouth into a smile, opened the door, and in my most enthusiastic tone of voice said, "Good morning, gentlemen. I'm so happy to see you."

After the technicians had arranged the lights and cameras, Morley Safer and I sat on the living room sofa. The little red light came on, the interview began, and I noticed that the cameraman was firmly planted on the turpentine-drenched spot. Throughout the program, I could see him sniffing the air as if confused by the strange, pungent odor. I didn't know if the carpet would dissolve, if the camera would short-circuit, or if the technicians would faint from the fumes. But the show was a success; I kept up my enthusiasm and smiled right into the camera, never once allowing my real feelings to erupt.

Enthusiasm is not just contagious—it spreads like wildfire. Employees often reflect the personalities of the company's owners. A chief executive officer's enthusiasm and positive personality can permeate an entire organization. Furthermore, changes in management often precipitate changes in a company's personality.

If a new chairman is cold and pompous, for example, a company's formerly cheerful atmosphere may vanish. Of course, you don't have to be the CEO to influence co-workers. Your moods—good and bad—will inevitably be reflected by those who work with you. It's up to you to control those moods and not let them control you.

The Power of One-on-One Enthusiasm Works

We all know the powerful effect that enthusiasm has on groups of people, resulting in hysteria at football games, sales pep talks, and political rallies. But most of our dealings with people are one-on-one relationships. Here the amount of enthusiasm we are able to generate is a measure of our powers of persuasion. And nothing is so persuasive as one-on-one enthusiasm. It may be expressed in many ways: body language, facial expressions, a nonverbal gesture, a twinkle in the eye, an "ear-to-ear" grin, or the tone of voice. I've talked by telephone with people who were halfway around the world—and felt the enthusiasm they generated. Salespeople who excel in telephone selling are proof that enthusiasm can be successfully transmitted by the voice alone.

Conversely, a lack of enthusiasm can produce devastating results. Hesitation and self-doubt are also contagious. Have you ever watched a salesperson who seemed totally indifferent to his own product? If a customer asks how the object functions or whether or not replacement parts are available, and the salesperson replies, "I don't know," or "I suppose so," this lack of enthusiasm is immediately transferred. Even a customer who enters the store eager to buy can be dissuaded from the purchase. Likewise, a manager who halfheartedly presents a new project to her people is likely to receive little support.

It's interesting to note that the word *enthusiasm* comes from a Greek origin meaning "God within." Similarly, enthusiasm must begin *within you;* when you are consumed with enthusiasm, those around you cannot help but respond in kind.

Independent National Sales Directors Talk about Mary Kay Principles in Action Today

As a graduate of Russia's Geological Institute and in a profession largely dominated by men, **Elena Romanova** was in no hurry to return to her work after becoming a mother. And even though no one took her seriously when she first decided to pursue a Mary Kay business, now, after having earned the use of three career cars and traveled the world, there's no doubt. It's easy for Elena to be enthusiastic, she says, when she sees all the lives she's been able to touch. "It's not about the amount of my commission or the cars, but about having an opportunity to help other women change their lives for the better!"

"No matter what Mary Kay was going through, she put a smile on her face. Her examples of how she handled adversity were my guide," says **Cindy Williams** of the United States, who talks of learning to walk on the sawdust dance floor where her mother worked. "I love Mary Kay's find-a-way, make-a-way spirit and was so inspired to be like her when she said she'd take 'I CAN over IQ' any day!"

"I'm a mediocre golfer, but one day I partnered with a woman who didn't know about my Mary Kay business. She was very excited and began to ask questions about my pink Cadillac, etc. When it was my turn to hit the ball off the tee, vavoom, it went further than it ever had before. I ended up with a par on the par 4 hole. She kept enthusiastically asking me questions about Mary Kay, and time after time, I had yet another fantastic shot. You have to understand, I never do that well. I believe it was a direct result of that positive energy she was giving me through her enthusiasm about my business," says **Nancy Sullivan** of the United States, who further believes, "There is nothing that works better than enthusiasm about your business. It's the main key to our success."

"People are enthralled to a purpose when the leader displays great enthusiasm and belief in presenting it. I remember times driving to a meeting when I physically didn't feel motivating at all. I would remind myself to 'act enthusiastic and you will become enthusiastic,' and it always worked," says **Kay Elvrum** of the United States.

9 The Speed of the Leader Is the Speed of the Gang

"The speed of the leader is the speed of the gang" is frequently heard at Sales Directors meetings. We believe a good Sales Director should set the pace for her unit. A Mary Kay Independent Sales Director who's working the way we've taught her will constantly encourage her people to strive for excellence in all facets of the business. She will emphasize that her unit members should become informed about the entire cosmetics field, master the product line, recognize the value of good personal grooming, serve the customer, and practice effective time management. Any leader can talk about excellence; a good one, however, leads by example.

Lead by Example

For instance, it's imperative for all Beauty Consultants to become thoroughly knowledgeable about our product line. This isn't unduly complicated; it's simply a matter of doing your homework. But a Sales Director can't convince her Beauty Consultants to become product experts unless she herself is an expert. I can't imagine a Sales Director conducting a sales meeting without thorough product knowledge. The admonition to "do as I say, not as I do" will not fly.

I'm sure it's the same in our Company as in others—nothing takes the place of a good, working leader. Unfortunately, many people who work hard to be promoted to a leadership position develop acute "executivitis" once they're promoted. Some members of the independent sales force stopped holding skin care classes after they became Independent Sales Directors. As a consequence, some became weak sellers, team-builders, and trainers. The success they had enjoyed in growing their businesses was the direct result of meeting new customers and prospective Beauty Consultants at skin care classes. Now glued to their desks, they no longer seemed to meet suitable prospects, and they couldn't imagine why! What's more, once they stopped working their businesses, they no longer inspired their unit members to do so. Have you ever noticed that your enthusiasm is always stronger when you have just *done* what you are to teach?

A leader must present a good example in appearance as well as work habits. Image is important. We're in the beauty business, so we always want to project a good image. Independent Beauty Consultants are self-employed, independent business owners. Therefore they have the right to wear whatever they choose. So again, it's up to the Sales Directors to lead by example. When a Sales Director dresses impeccably, this clearly reminds people that proper dress will enhance the image of a beauty expert. I take pride in the fact that women who represent Mary Kay have always followed this practice. As for myself, even if I must make a quick weekend or late-night stop at the office, I have always been very particular about what I wear because I feel it's important for me to set an example.

I also refuse to receive visitors to my home unless I look my best. As Founder of a cosmetics company, I feel I must project a certain image. And for this reason, if I'm not presentable, I simply will not answer my door. I've even had to limit a favorite pastime—gardening. I don't feel it would be appropriate to be seen in my yard covered with mud.

These practices have become well known, and as a result, I've been told that many National Sales Directors behave in the same manner. Every one of them dresses very smartly and is a style-setter for the thousands of Independent Beauty Consultants in her area.

Even the men in our Company are influenced by the dress of our male leaders. Several years ago, when Richard was still in his twenties, he decided that he wanted to wear sports shirts to work instead of suits. Within a matter of weeks, all the other men in the office had stopped wearing suits and were wearing sports shirts. When he realized what had happened, Richard returned to a more appropriate work image and shortly thereafter the other men did as well.

People frequently mimic a leader's work habits and self-discipline—for better or worse. If she habitually comes to work late, takes long lunch hours, makes long personal phone calls, has constant coffee breaks, and watches the clock all day, the people under her will probably follow that example. Fortunately, workers also copy the good habits. I make it a practice to clear off my desk at the end of the day and take unfinished work home in what I call my "think bag." I prefer beginning a new day with all previous work out of the way. Although I've never asked them to do so, my assistants and support staff now take "think bags" home too.

Operate from Experience

A good leader operates not on theory, but on experience. Simple directives may go unheeded unless you can back them up with ample proof that what you're asking others to do *can* be done. And what better proof than for them to know that *you* can do it? This was the rationale behind an interesting plan that was to cause quite a stir at Mary Kay. We had asked Independent Beauty Consultants to book 10 beauty shows for one week. We knew that if they held two shows every day, they would realize a dramatic increase in earnings. And so, on the way home from a Leadership Conference, members of our administrative staff designed a plan to accomplish this goal. At the next staff meeting, I sensed that something was in the air. Finally, it became apparent that the newest member had been elected to tell me something.

"Mary Kay," he said with much enthusiasm, "we have a fantastic idea, and we know that it's one you're going to love!"

With this he rose and began pacing around the room with the excitement of an expectant father.

"You're just going to love it," he repeated. "It's a great idea, and we know that it's going to work."

"What is it?" I asked calmly.

"Well, Mary Kay—we decided that if *you* held 10 classes in one week, then every Consultant and Sales Director in the field would know that if you could do it, with all you have to do, they could too!"

He glanced at the others before carefully adding, "Would you do it?"

I hadn't held 10 classes in 10 *years*, and so this was a shocking prospect. I rapped my fingernails on the conference table.

"The Lone Ranger never had hooves so loud," he said as he sat down.

But I was thinking that if I did it, no one else could have any doubts that she could do it as well.

"It's a great idea," I said aloud. "I'll do it."

It was later that the panic set in. How was I going to find 10 people for 10 classes? I didn't have any friends who hadn't already hosted several skin care classes. If they hadn't hosted a show, then they probably were no longer friends. The answer suddenly seemed obvious. I turned to our young spokesman and asked, "Phil, you're new with the Company; has your wife, Carol, ever held a Mary Kay skin care class?"

"Well, no. She hasn't," he replied.

"Fine. You tell Carol that I'm going to be calling her. She's going to just love this new experience."

I looked at the rest of the executives sitting around the table, and in a matter of minutes, I found several whose wives had never held a Mary Kay skin care class—including my daughter-in-law, the wife of the president of the Company. What amazed me was how hundreds of Independent Beauty Consultants had passed the offices of these administrators and had never thought to ask, "Has your wife ever held a Mary Kay skin care class?"

And so I accomplished what seemed at first an impossible job simply by looking in the most obvious place. I looked to those around me.

The sales department made quite a promotion out of it all. A contest was held to see who could hold the most shows, do the largest sales volume, and book the most future shows. In order to make sure that I'd get my 10 shows in, I actually booked an extra four. I even lined up my stockbroker for Saturday afternoon to show our men's skin care line.

Booking shows proved to be the easiest part of the task. What everyone had forgotten was that the product had evolved considerably over the previous 10 years. Of course, I had been involved with these changes, but I had never practiced the mechanics of

selling all the new shades or charting variances in skin tones. I
didn't even know how to assemble our fancy new display case!

So I contacted LaQueta McCollum of Dallas, and she
became my Sales Director for the promotion. She instructed me
on all the new products and helped me fill out an order for
merchandise. That requisition totaled $4,000.

LaQueta began her Mary Kay business in 1965, and
is an Independent National Sales Director Emeritus. In
surveys they completed for this book, many National Sales
Directors mentioned this very anecdote in describing
Mary Kay's hands-on leadership style.

I was astonished at the amount, and I said, "LaQueta, if I were
to take this home to my husband and tell him that I was going to
sell this much, he would tell me that I had lost my mind!"

"No," she insisted. "Trust me; I know you can do it."

The weekend before my "trial," I unpacked $4,000 worth of
Mary Kay® products. It included every shade of every product we
offered. I was overwhelmed by the physical scope of the line, and at
the same time, I was frightened. The sales department had
already announced in *Applause*® magazine that I had accepted the
challenge. Thousands of Independent Beauty Consultants were
now asking themselves, "Can she really do it?" And if I couldn't do
it, how would I recover from falling on my face in front of my
entire organization? They could never again trust what I had to say.

I practiced for hours, drilling myself on the details of every
item. I read the latest literature. I reread the educational manuals
that had been written long ago.

On Monday morning, I began the first class at the home of
my daughter-in-law. At this point you may be saying, "Of course,
she succeeded, she's the Founder of the Company. Who wouldn't

come to a show and buy cosmetics from Mary Kay herself?" But I had asked each hostess *not* to tell her guests that I would be presenting the program. And believe me, few recognized me, and none bought simply because I was Mary Kay. They gave me all the same excuses and resistance that every other Beauty Consultant receives: "I bought new makeup yesterday." "I don't need to cleanse my face with special product; I just use good ol' soap and water." "My husband lost his job, and my children seem to be coming down with chicken pox."

By the week's end I had held 10 shows, booked 19 for the future (which I subsequently turned over to someone else), recruited two new Beauty Consultants, and chalked up a sales volume totaling $2,500. When the top producers for the week were announced, I was actually number three in the entire United States! Considering I hadn't done a show in 10 years, that wasn't bad. It was a terrific feeling to know that I could still go out there and do it. And our corporate sales team was right; it *was* a wonderful morale booster for the sales force.

I'm sure there's not a sales manager around who hasn't heard "Things are different now from what they were when you were out in the field." This is probably the oldest cop-out on record. I'm sure the world's first sales manager heard this from the world's first salesperson. Naturally, things do change in time, but the basics of every business remain constant. There's nothing quite so inspiring to a sales staff as a leader who demonstrates that she or he still has what it takes to sell.

Through the years, Mary Kay Independent Beauty Consultants have had the flexibility to share Mary Kay products with customers through beauty shows—as Mary Kay Ash referred to them in this story—as well as skin care classes and color parties.

Showing Works Better Than Telling

Years ago, when I was a national training director for another direct-sales company, I traveled all over the country conducting sales meetings. When I had a morning meeting, I'd sometimes arrive the day before and hold a party for one of the salespeople. The next day when someone would say, "That worked 10 years ago, Mary Kay, but things are different now," I'd reply with an example, "It worked last night with Maria. It earned $200 for her. And that was right here in Boston, not Houston." It gave me tremendous credibility.

And so your image as a leader is based upon many complex factors: your knowledge of the company's product, your personal credibility and sense of self-respect, your sound work habits, and your willingness to demonstrate a thorough understanding of the workers' problems. But if you also happen to be a woman, then you can have additional challenges.

Women leaders from other industries sometimes ask me, "Mary Kay, how do you handle problems with men who resent the fact that you're a woman—and their boss?" Another question I frequently hear is, "What about *women* who resent having a woman as their leader?" I first tell them that I've never had that problem. But I do understand that other women do. "It doesn't make any difference what you are," I say. "You can be seven feet tall and purple, but if you can prove you know what you're talking about, you'll have the respect you deserve." Yes, a woman might have to work harder than a man to prove how good she is. But then, what else is new?

And finally, one of my pet peeves is the leader who doesn't use his or her own product. I have seen Cadillac dealers driving Mercedes and life insurance managers who were uninsured. Not only is it poor public relations, but it also has a most negative impact

on company employees! I believe that a leader should use his or
her company's products and do so with pride. I noticed that one
of our executives had been using another company's compact and
lipstick. One day while she was retouching her makeup, I went to
her desk and said quite dramatically, "Good heavens, *what* are
you doing? You can't possibly use that in this office!" Although I
said it with humor, she got the message. Later that day, I sent her
our lip and eye palette. Today all new employees are given a product demonstration and a complete set of Mary Kay® products.
And, of course, they are allowed to purchase any future needs at a
discount. I believe we must practice what we preach!

It really pleases me when I see a stranger using our products.
Recently I was on an airplane, and a woman three rows away
from me took out one of our lip and eye palettes as the plane
began to descend for the landing. I said to the flight attendant,
"Would you please tell that lady that I said thank you." Although
the attendant looked at me rather strangely, she passed along the
message. The woman turned to look at me, and I moved my lips
to thank her again. When the plane landed, she waited for me to
get off. She said that she recognized me and told me how much
she enjoyed our products. Naturally I was flattered, but I was also
proud. I believe in our products so strongly that I not only use
them myself, but I also enjoy sharing them with my family
and friends.

There's a great deal of responsibility involved with being a
leader. And the higher your position, the more attention you must
devote to projecting an appropriate image. You are always in the
spotlight, and you must act accordingly.

Lead by example, and soon your people will do as you do. All
the people at Mary Kay Inc. and in the independent sales force
believe that "the speed of the leader is the speed of the gang."

Independent National Sales Directors Talk about
Mary Kay Principles in Action Today

"People will come and work alongside you if you're working. Or they'll sit down with you if you're not," says **Bettye Bridges** of the United States. "The consequence of learning this is that I'm a better mother, a better daughter, and a better wife. Mary Kay is the greatest self-help program in the world."

"I cannot lead people to a place where I have never been," says **Liliana Actis Milanesio de Stettler** of Argentina.

Olena Romanova of Ukraine was a typical homemaker who discovered untapped leadership potential in herself. "Mary Kay showed me that I can be ambitious, that I can set goals; I can dream and I can work. The main secrets are to keep a positive attitude, develop the ability to communicate with people and take them as they are. We teach people by our own example—the speed, the goal, the results."

Taiwan's **Grace Kao** says, "The leader's speed is the gang's speed." For 16 years, she has used this Mary Kay truism to learn not only how to be a positive thinker but to become adept at turning challenges into opportunities. *The Mary Kay Way*, she says, has, "become the way of my life. It taught me to be positive and care about people."

The **Kazakhstan** National Sales Directors, successful businesswomen who remain true to their modest and shy roots, responded to our survey with group answers. As they explained, "It's impossible to teach playing the piano if you can't do it yourself. Only after working in this business can you teach others. Then you know the route, obstacles along the way, and how to overcome them."

10 People Will Support That Which They Help to Create

An assistant vice president with one of our competitors once approached me for a job. "I'm on a dead-end street, Mary Kay," he lamented. "Our company is going nowhere, and I don't feel there's any future for me there."

After we had talked for a while, I discovered his real complaint. The company was in the process of revamping its marketing strategy, and he had not been invited to serve on the committee that consisted of, as he put it, "the company's top brass." Now he vehemently opposed every single change that was being adopted. He went over each item point by point, explaining to me why he could not support it. But the company's revisions struck me as sound strategy. I couldn't help but conclude that the *real* problem was that he had not been asked to participate in the change. Had he been a part of the committee, I felt he would have been supportive. He was a bright young man who probably could have made a valuable contribution to the company, but instead his apathy was driving him to quit his job. A good man's ego had been bruised. Everyone has an ego. And like it or not, every leader must consider this fact before making any decision involving the people who work for him.

Ego is also a consideration when decisions involve those further up in the corporate structure. During the energy crunch of the '70s, I heard about a manufacturing company that was exploring ways to reduce its overhead. When it was brought to the attention of the budgeting committee that all of the executives were flying first class, the suggestion was made that in the future only individuals above a certain level should be permitted this luxury. The committee surveyed its executives, and their reaction was emphatic. They felt that the practice would result in a class system, dividing the management into first- and second-class executives—the haves and the have-nots. Elimination of the first-class "privilege" would create resentment among those to whom it was denied. Based upon the survey's conclusion that morale would suffer, the company continued to permit all its executives to fly first class and decided to explore other ways to reduce overhead. But the survey had served as a dramatic imperative to the executives that they *must* reduce company overhead. As a result many of them offered alternative ways to cut costs. In fact, their suggestions represented much greater savings to the company than would have been realized by eliminating first-class flying privileges.

We resist change, even when we are unhappy with the old way of doing things. I've seen people complain vigorously about an old system yet speak out strongly against any recommendation for improvement. After all, change does require people to act differently, to make adjustments, to do something differently. For many it's much easier to go along with the status quo.

When change is necessary, the way in which you present your case can make a world of difference in the kind of reaction that results. By involving others in the decision—by listening—you can not only avoid bruising egos, but you can raise their levels of self-esteem as well.

However, there is a downside to personnel involvement. The more people who are consulted, the greater the chance that confidential information may be disseminated outside your organization. Increasing the number of those involved is also more time-consuming, so implementation of the change may be delayed. Despite these risks, there is an enormous trade-off in high morale. I think it's of such importance to get people involved in those things that directly affect them that I've always been willing to take the gamble. If you want the full support of your people, you must get them into the act—the sooner, the better.

People Naturally Resist Change

I worked for a company whose owner decided to revise the commission schedule paid to his sales manager. All brochures and company literature were changed accordingly. He then made plans for personally announcing the changes during a series of regional sales conferences. I accompanied him to the first conference. I'll never forget it.

To an audience of 50 sales managers, he announced that the 2 percent override they were presently earning on their units' sales production was to be reduced to 1 percent. "However," he said, "in lieu of the 1 percent, you will receive a very nice gift for each new person you recruit and train." With that, he lifted a white tablecloth that had been covering a few small appliances such as clock radios and tape recorders. "You can choose any one of these," he continued, "and the more salespeople you train for the company, the more valuable the gifts you will receive."

At that point a sales manager stood up and let him have it with both barrels. She was absolutely furious. "How dare you do this to us! Why, even 2 percent wasn't enough. But cutting our overrides in half and offering us a crummy gift for appeasement insults our intelligence." With that she stormed out of the room. And every other sales manger for that state followed her—all 50 of them. In one fell swoop, the owner had lost his entire sales organization in that region—the best in the country. I had never seen such an overwhelming rejection of a change of this kind in my entire life!

The conference had begun on a Friday and was scheduled to last through the weekend. Instead, the owner flew back to Texas Saturday morning. Over the weekend he ordered reprints of the sales literature, thus restoring the original 2 percent override. On Monday we attended the next scheduled conference as if nothing had happened. But the sales organization in that region was gone, and not a single one of them ever came back!

That blunder taught me an invaluable lesson about change and how people resist it! People don't like giving up what they've already got. But there is also a more fundamental resistance toward action of *any* kind. Resisting change simply because it's new and different seems to be a natural human response. We become complacent all too easily, and thus change requires a conscious effort.

The book and record clubs business has thrived on the fact that most people avoid taking action. Every month these clubs send their members a card that must be returned if the member does not want to make a purchase. In other words, they have to take action in order *not* to buy! It's called the "negative option." It's easier to buy than to make a decision not to buy.

Seek Support from All Those Affected

A classic example of how people resist even a change for the better occurred once when we revised the structure of the independent sales force. Briefly, we elevated the status of a team leader (an intermediate position between Independent Beauty Consultant and Independent Sales Director) by increasing her rate of commission. In addition, upon reaching a certain plateau in sales volume, she earned the use of a car. This car was lower-priced than the one available to Sales Directors. But both the car and the team leader's new status would have provided excellent incentives for those women working their business at that level.

There was no question that the team leaders would welcome the new policy. Likewise, we anticipated a positive reception from the Independent Sales Directors because when their team leaders are motivated to increase sales, the Sales Directors also profit. (Let me add that the increased commissions and car bonuses would be a company expense.) How could anyone in the field *not* be ecstatic over those changes?

Yet there was resistance! We first presented the new program at a conference held in Dallas. But by the time we were able to relay the plan to the other regions of the country, "the grapevine" had carried misinformation to several Sales Directors. They feared that by expanding the team leader's position we were diminishing the role of the Sales Director. Once we met with them and clarified the program, however, it was enthusiastically received. People will support that which they help to create. Keep this in mind whenever you propose changing the status quo. In this case, we had worked very closely with *National* Sales Directors but we had not included Sales Directors who felt threatened by the change.

I suppose an alternative to making such important announce-
ments of change could have been to simultaneously make these
presentations "live" (via satellite and closed-circuit television) in
theaters and auditoriums across the country.

At the Company, we want our people's ideas. We encourage
them and openly solicit them. Their participation is vital to our
growth and health. The more that people are permitted to participate in a new project, the more they'll support it. Conversely, the
more they are excluded, the more they will resist it.

Perhaps the best way to introduce change in a business is to
keep one foot firmly planted on fundamentals and the other foot
searching for better ways to streamline operations. While it's vital
to examine potential changes carefully, in the majority of cases
you should stick to the basics. In our business, we've developed
many complementary cosmetic items, such as cheek color and lip
liner pencils in the latest colors and shades. But we always remember that our strongest suit is skin care. Though every company
must be innovative, no company dare allow its foundation to
crumble in hurried attempts to adapt to change.

In fact, during the past 20 years, Mary Kay has made no major
changes to its marketing plan. While competing companies offer
hundreds or even thousands of products, we've always tried to
limit the number of products we sell so that independent sales
force members can be knowledgeable about every item.

Our goal is to support the independent sales force with
products that are competitive, on-trend and relevant in the
ever-changing marketplace. To accomplish this, our
research and development groups focused on the identifica-
tion of scientific technologies that could be utilized to create exciting, new, and unique products or product benefits.

We choose the best of these technologies and then use them either to refine and upgrade our existing products— or, if more appropriate, create an entirely new product. The product range is kept as uncomplicated as possible. Regardless of whether an existing product is upgraded or an entirely new product is created, the goal is to explain the product and its benefits in a manner in which the independent sales force can easily understand. This helps to ensure that they have confidence in the product and feel comfortable explaining its benefits to their customers.

When we do introduce a new product, we often draw on the suggestions of the independent sales force. With hundreds of thousands of Independent Beauty Consultants who use and sell Mary Kay® skin care and cosmetics products to millions of women, there is no lack of ideas. Every week, numerous ideas are scrutinized by the marketing team. The team then requests feedback from various members of the independent sales force. With this feedback, concepts are presented to other departments, including R&D, manufacturing, and legal. The aim is to get as many people involved as possible.

One idea taken through this process involved a modification of our foundation. Research in the cosmetics industry has long recognized that this single product enjoys the greatest level of consumer loyalty. Therefore a resistance to change—either from Beauty Consultants or customers—could have had significant impact upon our position in the marketplace. Seven thousand individuals within the independent sales force directly participated in the testing and evaluation of the proposed change. When people participate to this extent, it becomes *their* project. When it's their project, the reception is much better than if we had simply presented a new product to them and said, "Here, go out and sell this."

Too many companies do just that—and it doesn't work! Too many leaders tell their people, "This is what we want you to sell. We'll take care of the rest." No matter how viable the proposals may be, such an attitude creates resistance. People want to feel that they have contributed to those things that affect their lives. When they don't, they feel slighted and manipulated.

It reminds me of the initial reaction of a husband whose wife arrives home and announces that she has invested the family savings in the stock market. Chances are he will not accept the validity of the decision since he was not consulted. A woman might react in much the same way if her husband were to "surprise" her by accepting an invitation to share their summer vacation with friends. Had she been consulted, she might have loved it, but since he acted alone, she is resistant.

We often implement ideas that come from consultation with our people. I remember one such instance that actually began as a personnel *problem*. I had an office employee who often came to work a few minutes late. She was an excellent worker, but in a year's time those lost minutes every day added up. No matter how often I asked her to be punctual, she continued to arrive late. I finally had to *insist*, with the clear implication that her position was in jeopardy.

"Mary Kay, I just can't get to work by 8:30," she explained. "I have four children to get up, feed breakfast, and get to school, and my youngest child doesn't leave the house until 8:30."

We discussed the problem, and I asked if she had any suggestions. "If I could just come to work at 10 every morning and work until 6," she said. "That way I could see my children off to school and avoid rushing to work." This was long before the acceptance of flextime, and I thought it was a very creative idea, which we were then able to accommodate because of our small size.

We had a real problem, and I encouraged her to share in the process of finding a solution. Had I simply announced a change in her working hours, she probably would have resented the idea and her work might have suffered. Instead she was very supportive, and there was never again a problem with her arriving late for work.

Seek Support from Above *and* Below

Good leaders are also well-advised to seek the support of upper management. Just as a manager might ask her staff "What do you think?" or "What do you want?" she is wise to seek feedback from managers above her. For example, she might say to her boss, "I need your help. You've been in this business a long time, and your insight would be very valuable." It's amazing how favorable people respond when their advice is sought (and how valuable their advice can be). Throughout their careers, leaders should continue to seek the advice of mentors: "What do you think about this?" or "We did as you suggested, and it's working fine, but here's another problem that needs your guidance." It's hard to imagine *not* having somebody's support when that person has given you advice from the birth of an idea to its completion. Here's a word of caution, however: Whenever you seek your manager's advice and don't follow it, be sure to communicate your reasons for not doing so. And again, invite her or him to participate.

When I say everyone likes to be included in new projects, I include myself. Once, during a meeting, it was announced that a change in one of our products was being considered. As our marketing person explained the change, I sat there feeling very foolish because I had no previous knowledge of this. At the next recess, I approached the staff member and asked her, "Why didn't anybody ever tell me about it? This is the very first time I've heard about this proposed change."

"You were consulted, Mary Kay. I mentioned it to you about a year and a half ago."

"A year and a half ago?" I replied. "I have no recollection of it."

"I'm sorry," she apologized, "but you were very busy at the time, so I didn't consult with you after that one brief encounter."

While her intentions were good, my immediate response was to play devil's advocate and give all the reasons why the idea wouldn't work. I found myself fighting it. Why did I react this way? Because I, too, support what *I* help to create—like everybody else!

Women and Change

People will sometimes remark that since the independent sales force consists primarily of women, we must experience greater resistance to change than other companies. I think it's grossly unfair to assume that women resist change more than men. In fact, I think the very opposite can be true. Today when a woman reaches middle age and her children have left home, she is often ready for a major change in her lifestyle. She may feel as though she's fulfilled the traditional role of raising a family and will begin to think in terms of another career. Creatively she's on an upswing at the same age the typical male has reached a stage where he may be on a downward slide. Often he becomes security-conscious, and the very thought of a major career change terrifies him. Instead he may be more interested in staying where he is, with an eye toward retirement.

However, I do believe it's especially important to confide in women. The fact is that many women leaders feel that they have previously been excluded from the "good old boy network" that exists behind the closed doors of some organizations. Many women have confided to me that they are concerned because the men in their organizations are privy to certain information not available to female leaders. While in many cases such concerns are more imaginary than real, they do, in fact, exist and should be addressed. With this in mind I recommend making an extra effort to involve women leaders in the early stages of any new project. This is a principle I have always followed, and women seem to thrive on it.

Being adaptable to change is an admirable quality in anyone—male or female—who hopes to succeed in business. Nevertheless, I believe that change is not necessarily progress. Change for the sake of change may improve nothing but your chance of being disappointed. If change is definitely called for, however, meet the situation head-on. Consider all options carefully, weigh the pros and cons, then adopt whatever course of action seems best. If no option seems feasible, leave things as they are until a better way presents itself. Why leave home if you have no place to go?

At Mary Kay, we *do* carefully consider change. Furthermore, we know that people react favorably to whatever changes they help to create. Even though today the Mary Kay independent sales force is one of the largest in the world, we make every effort to enlist their full support before introducing a new product. Sometimes it may delay the introduction of that product—longer perhaps than we'd prefer. But we're willing to live with a delay because we believe it's so important for people to feel involved in the decision. By the time that product is launched, it has become *their* product!

Independent National Sales Directors Talk about
Mary Kay Principles in Action Today

Mary Kay's friend came to the company's first location in 1963 to help her hang drapes, and she stayed to become the first Independent Beauty Consultant, first Independent Sales Director and one of the two first Independent National Sales Directors. **Dalene White** of the United States believes, "Promoting people from within assures a true understanding of the product, as well as the people, the purpose, the politics, philosophy, and culture."

From a pioneer to one who's among the youngest, this feeling is echoed. "In our business, it's important to find out what it is that makes someone tick. People will work hard for their *own* passionate purpose. Not yours, but theirs," says **Dacia Wiegandt** of the United States. She's also adapted one of Mary Kay's techniques from Chapter 6 as a verb. "I sandwich all the time to help people grow."

"It is easier to do what we understand," said the National Sales Directors from **Kazakhstan**, in their collective response to our survey. "Self-presentation allows us to understand and to be proud of our businesses. When you hold a study of successful companies, you come to understand that it is the people who make it that way. It was Mary Kay's belief that, 'When you find good specialists, make every effort to see that they stay.'"

"From the earliest days of the Company, Mary Kay made us feel as if everything would stop without us. We were part of the creation of the most talked about cosmetics company in the world," says **Carolyn Ward** of the United States, who is inspired to see this tenet passed forward.

"When we get to know someone who might be different from ourselves, when we try to understand her life experience, we grow. We pay attention to the merits of different characteristics so that we can appreciate and encourage each," says the highly successful **Nan Jiang** of China, who in developing her team has found "our hearts closely connect together. It's really a wonderful feeling!"

Sue Kirkpatrick of the United States used the technique when her children were young. "Each year after Seminar, we always sat down with our children and talked about goals for the new year. I enlisted their support. We have many fond memories of family involvement being instrumental in the success of my business. I believe that was a huge factor in our success. Everyone was working together—my team, their families, and my family."

11 An Open-Door Philosophy

My office door is always open—a standing invitation for anyone who wants to see me. The same is true for all of our corporate offices. On any given day we may have dozens of visitors, Beauty Consultants, and Sales Directors touring our Dallas headquarters. Occasionally we're startled by a quick flashbulb in a doorway, but we feel this is a small price to pay for conveying a relaxed and friendly atmosphere.

Doors Open Both Ways

Communicating our corporate image would be reason enough for an open-door philosophy, yet there is another more practical rationale for this. Doors open in two directions. Open doors also allow us the opportunity to truly know our people.

We are a "people-to-people," not an "office-to-title," company.

And so you won't find any titles on the doors of our corporate offices. My son, Richard, and I started this practice 20 years ago when we were the only executives. And if the chairman of the board and the president can still do without fancy nameplates, the other executives can manage too.

We also facilitate a friendly, relaxed atmosphere by addressing each other by our first names. I've worked for employers who, even after several years, insisted upon being addressed as "mister." I never thought such formality was necessary, so in my own business I have always insisted upon being addressed as "Mary Kay." Of course, when we began the Company, Richard was only 20 years old. He would have felt awkward being called "Mr. Rogers." But now, 20 years later, it's still Mary Kay and Richard to everyone.

Once a month, we welcome all new employees with an orientation meeting. We have the usual formal welcoming speeches, with various department heads explaining company benefits and policies.

For me the highlight is when I can spend an hour getting to know our newest staff members. I remember the early days when I was involved in the recruiting, hiring, and training of just about everyone. Now the groups are too large for me to individually process—and the intricacies of personnel administration are too complex. But people are still people, and my feelings of pride and responsibility for each new employee are just as intense today as they were for the very first person I ever hired.

Initially the group is very quiet and somewhat tense, not knowing exactly what to expect. I give them a short, warm greeting; then, in an informal way, I tell them the story of how our Company began. I always explain that our dream was to enrich the lives of everyone who works for the Company—not just financially, but emotionally and spiritually as well. And that's the way we still want it! I explain that we want them to enjoy their work, and that we always welcome their ideas and comments. After my brief comments, I invite them to tell me something about themselves.

Invariably someone will begin a question with, "Mrs. Ash, ..."

"Please, it's Mary Kay," I interject. "If you call me Mrs. Ash, I'll think you're either angry with me or don't know who I am. So, please, call me Mary Kay."

Later I'll tell them, "I don't want you to think of me as the chairman of the board; think of me as your friend."

Finally, just before they leave, I say, "If you ever need to talk to me, I want you to know that my door is always open."

Mary Kay Inc. maintains our Founder's strong belief that people are our most important asset. The Company continues this tradition established by Mary Kay Ash with a program dedicated to welcoming employees and sharing our corporate philosophy, customs, and traditions. Our three-day New Employee Orientation program has long been a critical factor in providing specific knowledge and influencing the attitudes of the newest Mary Kay employees. Reduced turnover, improved productivity, and stronger bonds are just a few of the benefits realized from helping new employees feel valued and able to assimilate to their new jobs more easily.

With hundreds of thousands of Independent Beauty Consultants, it's impossible for me to speak to everyone who has a question or a problem. For this reason, I have an administrative staff whose full-time responsibilities are helping me with correspondence and incoming telephone calls. My administrative assistants will first attempt to refer calls to the person most qualified to handle them. When a Beauty Consultant requests to speak to me, Jennifer Cook or Erma Thomson will ask the nature of the call, explaining that since the Company has grown so large, I can no longer personally handle everything. She then offers to transfer the call to the individual responsible for that specific area. However, if the call can be handled only by me, Jennifer or Erma will put it through.

A call I received from a young woman in Michigan illustrates such an occasion.

"Mary Kay?"

"Yes, this is Mary Kay. Is there something I can do for you?"

"Mary Kay, I'm depressed," the caller said.

I asked, "Is anything wrong? Is everything all right with your family?"

"No, no, nothing like that. I'm just not doing well in my business."

We talked for a while, and finally I told her, "Here's what we're going to do. We're going to have a special contest just for you. I want you to book 10 beauty shows for the next week, and after you've held them, I want you to call me back and tell me how you did."

"*Ten* shows?"

"That's right," I answered. "I want you to call each hostess in your date book and say that you just talked to Mary Kay. Tell her that I've established a contest for you, and then let her know how much you want to win it. Finally, ask her to be a hostess next week." Based on what she told me, I knew her problem. She was giving only one or two beauty shows a month. I also knew that former hostesses would be the most receptive to her request, giving her a better chance to book more beauty shows. With enough exposure, I felt she would do well. She just needed to gain confidence.

"Mary Kay, I'll try my best, but I just haven't been having much luck."

"You'll do fine," I assured her. "Now remember to tell them about the contest and that you've just talked to me. I'm expecting you to do well, and I want you to call me back so I will know how things are going. Good luck."

At the end of the following week, she called me back to report $748 in sales. Although it was not among the highest sales recorded that week, it was by far a record for her. Even though she hadn't booked all 10 shows, she was elated and seemed to have snapped out of her depression.

A Good Leader Should Be Part of a Team

Recently the husband of a National Sales Director was very ill, and I knew how upset she was. I called her at the hospital and said, "Right now your place is with him. Concentrate on doing everything you can for your husband, and don't worry about the business. You have some very capable women in your unit. They know the situation and are willing to work very hard on your behalf to show their love for you. You have our prayers, and I want you to know that whatever I can do for you, you have only to ask." I believe that when one is confronted by a family crisis, the family takes priority over one's career.

An employee once explained how much he appreciated working for a caring organization. "What a contrast to my previous boss," he confided. "One Saturday morning I was driving past his home, and I saw him mowing his lawn. My family and I were new in town, so I was happy to see a familiar face. I pulled into his driveway and rolled down my window to chat with him. 'How are you doing?' I asked him. 'How about that—we're neighbors. I live just two blocks over.'

"Before I could say another word, he said, 'Let's get one thing straight. Just because we work together doesn't mean that we socialize as neighbors. I never socialize with a subordinate, so it will be much appreciated if you don't stop by in the future.'

"Mary Kay," he continued, "I was absolutely devastated. And although he acted as if nothing had happened when I saw him at work the following Monday, I had lost all of my enthusiasm for the job."

I was appalled that one human being could treat another like that. All I could do was assure him that I was certain that no Mary Kay person would ever behave that way. "If it had been one of our employees, he would have offered to cut your grass after finishing his own," I added jokingly.

While it sounds hard to believe, some managers intentionally maintain a "closed-door" philosophy. I know a local Realtor who appointed his young, inexperienced son to serve as the firm's sales manager. Deciding that he would no longer be active in the residential end of the business, the Realtor instructed the agency's 22 agents to report directly to his son. The Realtor not only refused all telephone calls from the sales agents, but he locked his office door so he wouldn't be bothered with their visits. An agent who had been with the firm for 12 years told me of an encounter that took place as she and the Realtor were arriving for work. Innocently she asked him a question regarding the financing of a property she was trying to sell. He literally barked back, "Don't ever ask me a question. I don't even want to hear about the business. I have absolutely nothing to do with anyone in the office anymore."

The son, a chip off the old block, also kept his door shut, but for a different reason. The job was over his head. Feeling totally inadequate and insecure, he actually hid from the sales force. The firm's closed-door philosophy failed miserably. Within a year, the sales force had dwindled to three agents—the weakest three who couldn't find positions with any other real estate firm! The closed doors eventually forced the closing of what formerly had been a prosperous business.

I deeply care about the people with whom I work at our Company. Unlike many executives whose own insecurities make them feel uncomfortable about expressing warm feelings toward their associates, I don't believe in hiding mine. When the top executives of a large company feel that way, it filters down throughout the organization. For example, when I come to work each day, I always speak warmly to the security guards and to everyone else I see in the lobby. Even though our Company has grown so large that I can no longer call each by name, I have a warm greeting and a smile for everyone I meet.

Did you ever visit an office where nobody seems to talk to anyone? It's like being in a department store full of strangers. I have visited companies where people never bother to say hello and seem to go about their business ignoring one another. You'd never guess they were all working for the same company! In our building there's always conversation going on. "Hi there, how was your weekend?" or "How about those Cowboys on Sunday!" or "How did your daughter's birthday party go yesterday?" Even if they don't know one another, they're very likely to strike up a conversation!

It reminds me of when a man came into our reception area and took a seat without asking for anyone. The receptionist approached him and asked, "Sir, can I do something for you?"

"No, thanks, ma'am, I just came in here to recharge my batteries. You know, I call on offices all day long, and the people are often unfriendly. Sometimes they're downright ugly. But when I come in here, everybody is happy and smiling." He paused for a moment then added, "It's like coming into the sunshine; I just feel good all over."

It's like coming into the sunshine. I like that because that's what our open-door philosophy is all about. We want everyone who comes in contact with us to feel our warmth.

Independent National Sales Directors Talk about Mary Kay Principles in Action Today

Mexico's **Mireya F. de Narvaez** practices an open-door policy with her team, leading by example—even in the ladies room of a restaurant. "We were attending an event together chatting about Mary Kay when three women came into the restroom. They started asking about the products. Before we knew it, I had reservations for three classes. My team saw this. They learned," says Mireya. An avid reader who discovered Mary Kay in a business magazine story, she read this very book before deciding to pursue her Mary Kay business.

"In this business, we need to be warm, friendly, relatable, available, earthy, and genuine," says **Rena Tarbet** of the United States. "Aloof, arrogant, and removed are attitudes that just don't work," says the down-to-earth woman who's built a highly successful business while waging a 32-year battle with cancer.

Mary Kay Ash has been given plenty of credit for helping women succeed in business, all of it well deserved according to **Jean Santin**. "She taught us about business, but she also taught us to be givers. And that it was good to be a warm, kind, and 'from-the-heart' leader. Most of my days are spent helping someone not just in her business, but in her life."

12 Help Other People Get What They Want— and You'll Get What You Want

The most important justification for being in business is service to others. Every new business must be built upon this premise, since wanting to make money or desiring to "dabble" in a favorite pastime is not enough to sustain such a venture. The business must fulfill a need.

Everyone's job should focus upon this goal. So as leaders, our first concern must be helping others. And it follows that if your attention is directed toward helping others, you will be rewarded. I like to remind Independent Sales Directors of this truth when they ask me to autograph one-dollar bills as awards for their Independent Beauty Consultants. Next to my name, I write "Matthew 25:14-30," which is the parable of the talents. It tells us to use and increase whatever God has given us, and that when we do we shall be given more. I deeply believe in this philosophy, and I've always applied it throughout my business career.

When Mary Kay began, I wanted to create a company that would give women an opportunity to accomplish anything they set as their goal. It was equally important to create a product that would help people. Our skin care products do help women look beautiful on the outside and feel beautiful on the inside. I believed that if these two dreams could be accomplished, we would be successful. I believed so strongly that helping others was the most important motivation for starting a business that I completely ignored the advice of both my accountant and my attorney.

My accountant looked at the financial projections and said, "Mary Kay, your commission schedule will never work. It's only a matter of time before you'll be bankrupt!"

My attorney had the same advice: "Mary Kay, you have no experience in the cosmetics business, and you are a grandmother. Don't throw your life savings away!"

They were my financial experts, so I attentively listened to their advice. But I decided to go on. I wasn't being stubborn, far from it. I simply believed so strongly that helping others was a valid business principle that I was willing to stake my entire future on it.

Then and now, everything anyone in the independent sales force does to succeed is based upon helping others. Beauty Consultants help customers, and Sales Directors help their teams succeed. Our culture encourages each person to help others in order to climb the ladder of success. The individual who thinks only "What's in it for me?" will never make it in our Company. We truly believe that if you help enough other people get what *they* want, you will get what *you* want! In my view, the people who are the most successful are those who have helped the most people grow.

A Mary Kay Independent Sales Director is cheering for every woman in her unit to succeed. She shouldn't fear that someone on her team will outperform her and thereby threaten her career. In most businesses this is not true. Often the success of a worker can lead to his replacing his own manager. I know the manager of a local insurance company who lives in constant fear of this prospect. He knows that since he is in his late fifties he would have a difficult time relocating elsewhere. The company's philosophy is to hire only one manager in a given market—and they insist upon promoting from within rather than transferring someone from another territory. While the manager has always liked the idea that his company would never transfer him or move in someone to replace him, he now has two young star performers who want his job! Consequently, he does his best to discourage them from leaving sales and seeking a managerial position with the company. I suspect that in order to protect his job he would even harass them to the point that they would resign.

It's unfortunate when a company puts its people in such a position. In the long run, everyone loses—including the company. While there are still options, smart people should avoid entrapment and seek a company that encourages its people to help one another, thus enabling everyone to find fulfillment in his or her work.

Today's woman manager is too often painted as thoroughly calculating and absolutely ruthless, clawing her way up the corporate ladder and stepping on everyone in her path. Sometimes she is said to behave in this way because she feels insecure in a man's world; she's always on guard, always feels threatened. I think this image is unfair to women. Unfortunately, because it's still rare for a woman to be promoted faster than a man, everything she does in her job is accentuated. In my opinion, a hostile company environment will bring out undesirable qualities in both sexes. When a woman plays by the rules that men have set (as she usually must), her behavior is observed more carefully. "But a woman is not supposed to behave like that," you might hear from men, as well as women. To whatever extent such criticism is justified, I blame those companies that encourage "dog eat dog" behavior as a matter of policy.

Nice Guys Finish First

"Nice guys finish last." That familiar adage immortalized by the late baseball manager Leo Durocher implies a correlation between being nice and being a loser. Many people believe this cliché simply because it's been so often repeated. Unfortunately, it can become a self-fulfilling prophecy.

The media has distorted the image of modern business leaders, focusing on sensational exposés of white-collar crimes. The wonderful philanthropic deeds of our business leaders too often go unreported. Newspapers eagerly print the latest scandal on Wall Street but ignore the tremendous contribution to the town library or public park. Movies and television still perpetuate the image of the ruthless, mercenary, cigar-smoking businessman.

Consider the managers portrayed in most movies. Loudly and clearly the message comes across: Success and decency don't mix! It's the bad guys who manage business in America—with or without the smoking cigars.

Ask the man in the street for his opinion of business leaders, and his remarks are likely to be uncomplimentary. Yet ask him if he personally knows anyone who's headed a successful business and you may hear:

"Yes, I know the president of ABC Company."

"What kind of person is he?"

"Oh, he's a great guy."

"Anyone else?"

"The chairman of the board of XYZ Company. He's one of my favorite people."

And so, regardless of personal experience, the American public still perceives those who have climbed to the top of the corporate ladder with an unflattering abstraction. I believe this is a distortion of the truth. I personally know dozens of highly successful CEOs of major corporations, and the majority of them are honest, compassionate human beings. I truly believe that decent people are far more likely to succeed in business than scoundrels and bullies. A leader who mistreats people will end up managing a workforce of unmotivated, unhappy, negative people. And as their leader, he just isn't going to make it!

A Good Leader's Success Is Reflected in the Success of Her People

I can tell you that at Mary Kay a selfishly motivated Independent Sales Director will ultimately fail. To succeed with her business, she must think in terms of what's good for her people, not herself. If a Sales Director tries to manipulate people, it's a sure bet that sooner or later she'll fail. Her success, like the success of any leader, rests squarely upon the successes of her people. Only by truly caring for her Beauty Consultants can she make them *want* to improve their performance. And if they don't want to, they won't—it's as simple as that. While both men and women are strongly motivated by a caring leader, it's been my experience that women generally respond more quickly to this than do men. Perhaps it's a woman's sensitivity that makes her more responsive to caring treatment. She may be more likely to react from the heart rather than from the head.

Love—not profit—has often caused her team to display immense loyalty to a deserving Sales Director. For example, a new Sales Director suffered serious personal problems that for two consecutive months resulted in a production decline. Unless the sales volume in the third month improved, she was in danger of losing her Sales Director status. To make matters even worse, this occurred during January when a record-breaking cold spell had kept everyone housebound. By the end of the third week of the month, her sales production fell short.

This Sales Director is a delightful person who is loved by the women in her unit. Knowing the serious consequences if that final week's production fell any further, two of her Beauty Consultants took the initiative to call the other women in the unit. They explained that if everyone cooperated and did her share, the unit would remain intact. So out of deep loyalty to the Sales Director, the entire unit worked together to increase the unit's production.

Strong motivation of this sort, stemming from loyalty, often surfaces when fellow workers have strong emotional ties with a leader they respect and like. I emphasize the word *like* because obviously people won't rally around a leader in trouble if they don't like her! Loyalty isn't something a leader is automatically given. It doesn't go with the territory. It must be earned. So when times are tough, the person who isn't liked will not get the needed support from their team members. Instead, they may be rooting against him or her.

It's important to realize that being a "nice guy" doesn't mean that a leader is nice because he or she says yes to everything. A good leader must be able to say no when that's the only answer. But he should be tender as well as tough. For example, he can't award unwarranted salary raises merely to increase his popularity. But he cannot deny a request for a raise with loathsome accusations: "Not only will I *not* grant you a raise, but I don't even think you're worth what I pay you *now*." A better way to deny such a request might be to weigh the person's productivity against the company's needs and tactfully deny the raise on the basis of performance. Some people have a knack for saying no so considerately that the person to whom it is directed is not the least offended. These leaders might even add a touch of encouragement such as, "Let's sit down and review what you should do during the next 12 months to merit an increase in salary."

Some leaders avoid saying no because they don't want to hurt anyone. They do nothing—hoping that the problem will somehow disappear. But trying to avoid confrontation by giving in to people is not what good people management is all about. It's a sign of weakness. Perhaps *those* nice guys and gals do finish last!

Within well-operated, growing corporations good leaders can only prove their worth by helping others. Ideally advancement in such companies results from growth: opportunities becoming available as jobs open. Consequently good leaders must develop good people to fill vacancies due to promotions as well as those that are newly created. In this sense, a leader's success is reflected in the success of his or her people.

I believe the passage in Scripture that reads, "To whom much is given, from him much shall be required." A good leader knows that it's his job to help others within the organization. He also knows that the best way to help others is by making them strong—so they can help themselves. In fact, if you help people to the point where they become dependent on you, you're likely to end up hurting them—and they'll resent you for it!

There's an old story about Canadian geese that migrated thousands of miles each winter to a warm climate and returned each spring to the fields surrounding one small Canadian village. The villagers loved these beautiful birds and looked forward every year to their return. One spring, due to unseasonably cold weather, the ground was frozen and no food was visibly available for the wild geese. Anticipating their return, the townspeople scattered feed outdoors and built shelters. The intention was to help the geese to survive until spring-like weather appeared.

They were so delighted to see how readily the geese accepted their offering that they continued to feed them throughout the spring and summer. However, when fall came, the wild geese didn't fly south as they had always done in the past. Instead they had become so fat that their wings could no longer lift their heavy bodies off the ground. As the weather grew colder, they simply waddled into the shelters that the villagers had constructed; and as the story goes, they never flew again.

We want to help people, but we don't want to make the same mistake as the Canadian villagers. I always say that each Beauty Consultant must ensure her own survival. We help her accomplish this task through encouragement and through intense education.

Every Beauty Consultant has access to an in-service educational program that emphasizes product refinement, human relations skills, business procedures, and time management. In addition, we have developed a Pacesetter Class in which a Sales Director selects her most talented performers and helps them earn a very special Company bonus: the use of a VIP automobile. When a Sales Director has helped four Beauty Consultants earn the use of their cars, she has earned for herself the use of her own symbol of superiority: a brand-new pink Cadillac.

It was 1969 when the top five Independent Sales Directors received keys onstage to beautiful pink Cadillacs. Now, the Mary Kay Career Car program is legendary through-out the world. The program is so well recognized that a pink car says "Mary Kay," even to those who may know nothing else about the Company.

As I've mentioned, the ultimate award given to the top salespeople in our organization is a large, diamond-studded bumblebee. We think the bumblebee is a perfect symbol because, as aerodynamic engineers "proved" many years ago, the bumblebee cannot fly! Its wings are too weak, and its body is too heavy. Fortunately, the bumblebee doesn't know that and goes right on flying. At Mary Kay we teach people how to spread their wings and fly on their own. I can't think of a better way to help people.

Independent National Sales Directors Talk about Mary Kay Principles in Action Today

"Our success should result from the individual successes of the people we lead," says **Nan Stroud** of the United States, who has a poignant memory of the day Mary Kay visited her city. She was proudly driving Mary Kay to her home—only to find it on fire. "Her example of being a problem-solver that day made such a huge impression on me."

"Well, first of all, helping others succeed certainly never feels bad. If you know what people want and you can help them achieve that, in doing so, you grow yourself. It's the ultimate win-win situation," says Brazil's **Eloisa Johnson**, who left a successful Mary Kay business in the U.S. to pioneer in her native country, where she became the first NSD. "Mary Kay is so unique as an organization because the Founder and now her leaders understand the importance of every step and of rewarding accordingly."

At the Mary Kay corporate offices in Shanghai, quotes from top sales force leaders in China adorn the heritage area, a large wall that tells the story of the Company. Even in translation, their sentiments depict a reverence for the principles learned from Mary Kay Ash, illustrated in the quote from **Xin Ling Liu** of China who said, "Some integrated and kind-hearted people may not succeed, while some so-called successful people may not be integrated and kind-hearted. But the lives of those integrated and kind-hearted people are sure to be beautiful and perfect once they succeed."

"I've realized that it is more important to applaud and see my team receive recognition than it is for me to receive it. I feel very proud of that," said **Elena Martiniuc** of Moldova.

13 Stick to Your Principles

In business, everything is subject to change—people, products, buildings, machinery, everything—except principles. To paraphrase Thomas Jefferson, in matters of principle, stand like a rock; in other matters, swim with the current. So, while I strongly advocate flexibility, when it comes to principles we must stand firm.

But what if your principles are incompatible with those of the company for which you work? If so, a change is in order—either your company's principles or your job!

During my pre-Mary Kay days, I made several job changes because I opposed the principles of various employers for whom I worked. There were certain practices I simply couldn't live with. For one, I could not believe that a woman's brain was worth 50 cents on the dollar for doing the same work as a man. I also found it unacceptable for a deserving woman to be passed over for promotion simply because she was female.

I tried to see the other person's point of view, and I'm a realist—I had three children to support. With my family's welfare in my mind at all times, my first reaction was to try to understand and then try to influence my employer's attitude.

There are times when your personal principles might not be in harmony with those of your co-workers. But to seek other employment without first trying to resolve the problem would be to overreact.

What if your co-workers regularly use language that you find offensive, for instance. You still want to function in a friendly, smooth-running work environment, so what can you do? Complain? Sulk? Join in? I believe that the worst thing you could do would be to join in simply to be accepted by the group. This would be a serious compromise of your principles. Nor should you continually complain or act resentful. Rather I think you should let the others know that obscene language offends you and then proceed with your duties. By setting an example for your principles, you may gain the respect of someone else, thus encouraging him or her to follow your lead.

An actress I admire refused to do a nude scene in a movie for which she had contracted. After expressing her feelings about the scene to the producer, he agreed to cut it from the film. Her immediate response had not been to try to get out of her contract, but rather to try to make a change that was compatible with her principles.

The principles I'm discussing in this chapter are moral issues. Sometimes people use the word *principles* loosely when that really is not what they mean. A man might have an accounting background, and his manager asks him to be more sales-oriented. "I'm not a salesperson," he insists, "and I won't work in sales. *It's against my principles.*" The fact that an accountant doesn't want to be involved in selling has nothing whatsoever to do with principle. The same is true of a salesperson who says, "I object to filling out reports every day; *it's against my principles.*" Once again, the salesman's dislike of paperwork does not originate from his principles. I mention this important distinction only because so many people misuse the word *principle* to express a grievance that is nothing more than a like or dislike. You should not say that something is "against my principles" unless you mean that it is morally abhorrent to you.

Unfortunately when most people talk about principles, it is simply lip service. To me the morale of an entire company suffers when its leaders boast: "The customer always comes first," and then fail to practice it! Many managers and salespeople make this claim at the time of sale, but they cannot be relied upon for service *after* the sale. When employees see customers mistreated, their confidence is destroyed. Their sense of pride is injured, and it makes them feel ashamed to be associated with such practices. I believe that it's essential to "practice what you preach."

A Good Leader Should Be an Example to Others

Good leaders should be examples to others. Failure to abide by the principles they proclaim destroys the morale of their associates and undermines the leaders' credibility. It's the same way that the public feels about elected officials who are found guilty of criminal charges, for instance.

Our Company was founded on certain basic principles, and we've always taken pride in announcing them to the world. We were determined to offer a wonderful opportunity for women to earn as much as their abilities would allow. We have made a commitment to be the world's finest teaching-oriented skin care organization. And it is my belief today that no other cosmetics company in the world has as many highly qualified people. Hundreds of thousands of Beauty Consultants have truly become highly skilled in the field of skin care.

Treating People Fairly Makes Them Feel Secure

Another principle that we cherish is our practice of the Golden Rule. It's applied in every decision we make. People feel comfortable in the knowledge that they will always receive fair treatment from our Company. In fact, with an independent sales force of hundreds of thousands, we must take even greater pains to treat everyone fairly. Giving preferential treatment to some would cause bitter feelings and resentment throughout our entire organization. In many ways, I believe women are more sensitive than men to the presence or absence of fair play. Perhaps this is because women have so often been victimized. Consequently, since we have one of the world's largest independent sales forces and since that organization consists primarily of women, we're always alert to the need for equality. Women and men alike feel secure when they're treated fairly. And in our organization, they know they can depend upon it.

Our people also know that we are sincere when we tell them that our priorities are: "God first, family second, and career third." Yes, our leadership team does consist of hardworking, career-oriented people, but over the years we've demonstrated that God and family take priority over career. Members of many faiths are represented in our Company, and all religions teach us that we are placed on this earth to help our fellow man. Yet while I believe God has been instrumental in the growth of our business, I am careful to avoid preaching. Since our people represent all faiths, I never try to impose my personal religious beliefs on others. I do, however, let it be known that God plays a very important part in my life. I have always believed that when you put God first, your family second, and your career third, everything will work out. When the order of those priorities is changed, nothing seems to work!

Putting Family before Career

I believe that leaders must respect the sanctity of the family. And the only way you as a leader will ever let this priority be known is by demonstrating it as a family-oriented individual who truly loves his or her spouse and children. Yet it's not enough to love your family; you must also spend time with them and let them know that their happiness will never be sacrificed for your career.

I realize that there are those who scoff at this philosophy. To them, "work comes first." If a mother arises one morning to discover a seriously ill child, this kind of leader would say, "Get a sitter or make other arrangements. Your place is at the office." If a father asks to be excused one afternoon to watch a child be inducted into the National Honor Society, a callous boss would say, "There will be other award ceremonies." But I believe that it's wrong to ask anyone to abandon a sick child or forgo an important family milestone.

I have always functioned at a pace and with a God-given energy that would qualify me as a workaholic. But when I was raising my three children, *their* needs came before my job. You see, *they* were my motivation for working those long, hard hours. We encourage this same balance in the independent sales force.

I understand employers who wish to ensure that they will receive an "honest day's work" from every employee. But we trust people to be as fair and as responsible to their jobs as we are to ours. And so at Mary Kay, we are pleased when people place their careers in third place behind God and family. We believe this is the way it should be!

Not long ago the value of this principle was reinforced in a most personal way. Seven weeks before his death we were told that my own dear husband, Mel Ash, had cancer. It was a period that forever changed my life. Initially we didn't know the extent of his illness, and Mel encouraged me to continue my work as usual. But I didn't want to leave him. I would sit with him most of the day, and when he would nap, I would go to my desk and work on whatever was urgent.

A year earlier, I had been invited to speak at the General Federation of Women's Clubs Convention to be held in St. Louis. Thousands of people had already made reservations to attend, and I knew that they were counting on me. Mel said that he would be fine and that I should go. But I was torn between my responsibility to him and my responsibility to my commitment. Then I remembered my often-quoted principle—the foundation and cornerstone of our Company: God first, family second, career third. Independent National Sales Director Dalene White went to St. Louis in my place and represented me with grace and skill. But even without the availability of such a competent replacement, I felt my greatest responsibility was to my husband.

Responsibility to our customers is also of importance to our Company. Maintaining product quality is a principle honored at Mary Kay. Product excellence has always been a top priority and will always be one of the Company's major goals. We produce all our cosmetics to meet standards that are established for the drug industry, which are higher than those required for cosmetics. Although we are not required to comply with such stringent regulations, we prefer to subject our products voluntarily to the highest possible quality criteria. In the long run, lip service without performance is self-defeating, because it ultimately affects the public's acceptance of your product.

In a typical year, Mary Kay Inc. spends millions of dollars and conducts more than 300,000 tests to ensure that every Mary Kay® product meets the highest standards of safety, quality, and performance. Because we perform or supervise every step of the product cycle from inspiration and formulation to distribution, each new product must pass a series of stringent research and consumer testing procedures. Mary Kay scientists test for safety, quality, stability, purity, skin efficacy, product usage, performance and, of course, consumer acceptance. Mary Kay regularly goes beyond what is mandated by law when it comes to product safety.

Make Product Excellence a Top Priority

Not only do we take pride in our products, we offer a 100 percent money-back guarantee on all merchandise we sell. If a Beauty Consultant's customer is not completely satisfied and sends back the unused portion of a product, she'll receive a full refund. This is true even if the container is empty, or the Beauty Consultant who made the original sale is no longer with us, no matter what the length of time between date of purchase and request for refund.

We make outstanding products, so refund requests affect a very small percentage of total sales. Our refund policy is generous because we want customers to be happy and satisfied with the products and services they receive. We want the Beauty Consultants and Company employees to be happy and proud of what we do. If any one of them isn't happy, we all suffer. In our business, satisfying people's needs is what we're all about—it's another one of the principles we live by.

Independent National Sales Directors Talk about Mary Kay Principles in Action Today

"When I began my business, I was so excited because I knew if I completed the requirements, I could do well. In other work situations, it was popularity, tenure, and gender—even my youth at the time—that could hold me back. But not at Mary Kay," says **Anita Garrett-Roe** of the United States.

"The Golden Rule is the only true guarantor of success," says **Elvira Manthei** of Germany, a former government employee who has broken sales records and drives a pink Mercedes convertible.

"Character does NOT depend on circumstances," according to **Holly Zick** of the United States.

Says China's **Mei Gu**, "People grow to be great as a result of a great mission."

"All the things so crucial to the Company and its continued success are within this chapter. Outstanding character and unwavering judgment are good examples of what will continue to set us apart," says **Sherry Alexander** of the United States.

14 A Matter of Pride

Some time ago, a popular local columnist wrote an article for the front page of the *Dallas Morning News* that caused quite a furor among our people. While driving to work he had noticed a bumper sticker with the message, "Ask Me About Mary Kay Cosmetics." He said the woman driver was wearing a bathrobe, had her hair in rollers, and wore no makeup. "How could that woman tell anyone how to be beautiful?" he wrote.

The article appeared on a Monday morning, and by 7 A.M. my phone was ringing off the wall with the question, "Did you see the article about us on the front page?" Knowing that many Independent Beauty Consultants would be attending meetings in our building that morning, I had the article pinned to all our bulletin boards. Above it in big, bold print was the question: Was this you? Later we sent the article to independent sales force members all over the country asking them the same question.

Take Pride in Your Image

As leaders in the beauty industry, we take pride in our image. Obviously, the woman driving that car didn't think about her, or our, image. Members of the independent sales force agree they should always look their best when appearing in public. A Beauty

Consultant should make other women *want* to look beautiful, and she should set an example. Actually, the article worked to our advantage. Some people were shaken because the article brought to their attention the fact that they, too, were perhaps occasionally neglecting their appearance. I've always felt the effort a woman takes to look her best is one reflection of the pride she has in herself. And this particular expression of pride is essential if you are in the beauty business.

Happily, a strong sense of pride is already instilled in most people who decide to start a Mary Kay business. Although we do not stipulate that only attractive, well-groomed women are eligible, you might think so if you were to attend a sales force member's meeting. The Mary Kay independent sales force sets standards that will not tolerate a fellow sales force member who presents an unkempt appearance. If someone who becomes a Mary Kay Beauty Consultant does not initially share those standards, she usually works quickly to improve herself, or she leaves of her own volition.

Pride in one's appearance prevails in our manufacturing plants, too. Just as our plant workers take pride in their appearance, we are proud of our state-of-the-art facilities. We consider our manufacturing facilities to be an exemplary showplace in the cosmetics industry, and we're delighted when visitors ask for a tour.

Across the globe, more than 150 Mary Kay facilities occupy more than 3 million square feet of space. Company manufacturing plants in Dallas, Texas and Hangzhou, China, feature state-of-the-art packing lines, production areas, laboratories, and warehouses. While efficiency and functionality are key in meeting market demand, keen attention is also paid to image and pride. For example, the Dallas world headquarters building features a museum in its lobby, and the manufacturing plant in China features a wrap-around viewing corridor where visitors can watch the entire production process. There are also common areas in many Mary Kay offices around the world that reflect the Mary Kay culture and heritage.

Our manufacturing employees share in our Company pride because they know how much independent sales force members rely upon them to produce cosmetics of uniformly high quality. Any item that does not meet our specifications will not be sold. It hurts sometimes to see this merchandise destroyed, but it's necessary. If a product isn't of premium quality, it will not be sold.

We are proud of the competitive quality of our products, but we never express this pride as criticism for other cosmetic brands. We feel when you degrade a competitor's product, every knock is a boost for the other company. We believe not only that such criticism would reflect poorly upon our own degree of professionalism, but also that it's in direct conflict with our philosophy of conducting business by the Golden Rule.

Pride Contributes to Morale

A salesperson who works for a dress manufacturer told me how differently his company operates. "We show our line several months before the dresses are actually manufactured," he explained to me. "For this reason, special samples must be made so we can present the line. The quality of the samples is usually far superior to the final product, so the buyer receives merchandise that isn't nearly as well made as the dresses that were shown."

"This just kills everyone's morale," he continued. "We feel we're being deceptive. It's so embarrassing when a customer says,

'This isn't what I bought.' It goes much further, however, than just lowering the morale of the sales force. The entire company is affected. But the real blame belongs to management, who is willing to spend more money on samples than on the delivered goods." Such tactics exact a heavy toll from everyone's morale.

And the shame this clothing salesman felt even extended to his family. They, too, were embarrassed that he worked for an unscrupulous manufacturer.

One of the areas from which Mary Kay derives a great deal of pride is the esteem in which our families hold our Company. They are very proud to say that their children, mothers, or fathers are associated with Mary Kay. In letters to me, children of the independent sales force say such things as, "In only six years I'll be 18 years old, so I can become a Beauty Consultant like my mother."

Mary Kay Ash always felt a great sense of pride that so many women wanted to share their chosen careers as Independent Beauty Consultants with family members— aunts, nieces, sisters, cousins, and so on. In fact, over the years, many mothers and daughters have enjoyed growing their individual independent Mary Kay businesses—all the while learning from one another and supporting each other to achieve their own great success. Shirley Hutton and Elizabeth Fitzpatrick were the first mother-and-daughter Independent National Sales Director team. Shirley, now an Emeritus, debuted in May 1980; Elizabeth in July 1994.

There's nothing more rewarding than knowing you have put in a good day's work. There's an inner sense of pride from knowing you've done a first-rate job. It's the equivalent of that wonderful feeling you get from scoring high on an examination, sinking a 25-foot putt, making a perfect landing in an airplane, baking a delicious apple pie, or completing a beautiful oil painting. A leader should strive to instill a sense of pride in people, no matter what kind of work they do. Tradesmen, assembly-line workers, salespeople, and file clerks—as well as executives—enjoy being proud of their work. We all need praise now and then. An "I don't care" attitude quickly sets in if our best efforts go by unnoticed. Recognition makes us all feel good about our work and, consequently, ourselves.

An advertising agency executive showed me how we can instill pride in others. She had praised one of her artists for a particularly good layout he'd done. "Thank you," he told her, "but I think it needs a little touching up to be just right." He then spent his entire lunch hour working on it. "I had never known him to work through the noon hour," she said. "Yet because of that little word of praise, he suddenly became a perfectionist, striving to do an even better job."

All of our Company's activities are in the pursuit of excellence. No matter what we achieve, we are never completely satisfied; we're always searching for ways to improve. This pursuit of excellence exists in everything we do. Everyone associated with us knows that excellence is synonymous with Mary Kay Inc., and it is this pervasive attitude, I believe, that builds self-esteem in all people.

The word *excellence* is often bandied about so much that it has come to mean different things to different individuals. And so, for example, when our marketing people are working to create a new sales brochure, they must first agree on the specific qualities they wish to portray. What we're after is a standard of excellence. Without establishing a standard, the specific excellence we are seeking remains nebulous. But when a group of us gets together and exchanges thoughts, good ideas emerge, and these evolve into better ideas until a standard of excellence is established that's acceptable to the entire team.

I believe that when people strive for excellence as a team, everyone's level of performance is elevated. No one wants to let the others down. Everyone wants to contribute. When a leader instills this kind of pride in people, it becomes a major factor in improving their performance. The New York Yankees baseball team has a well-earned reputation for excellence. I've heard it said that when a player dons the Yankee's striped uniform, he plays better ball. Why? Because he's proud to be part of a team with a winning tradition.

Similarly the Cadillac is considered the hallmark of quality in the American automobile industry. For this reason, we award the use of pink Cadillacs to those Sales Directors whose units have attained a certain sales volume. Whenever people see a pink Cadillac, they know it's being driven by someone who has achieved personal success. The car inspires tremendous pride of ownership; you'll rarely see one dented or even dirty. In fact, the women are so proud of them that the cars are often parked in the driveway instead of the garage.

It's a Grand Old Flag

The pride we feel for our work and our Company is similar to that which we feel for our country. We are proud to be Americans, and we are proud to let everyone know it.

Several years ago, in his closing remarks at one of our annual Seminars, my son Richard verbalized our patriotism this way:

"Over the years, I have given many Mary Kay speeches related to our free enterprise system. I feel our free enterprise system is important because without it you would not be here. I would not be speaking. Mary Kay would not exist. And the Mary Kay dream would never have become a reality.

"Free enterprise means different things to different people. To me it means individual liberty, which implies individual economic freedom, as envisioned by our founding fathers. The earliest leaders of this nation were determined to set up a free citizenry rooted in the natural law of supply and demand with minimal state and federal interference. They envisioned the right of everyone to succeed or fail according to his or her own initiative, drive, and ability. Since that original dream of our founding fathers, we've come a long way as a nation. We have become much more sophisticated. We have grown and capitalized on the free enterprise system, and we have established a standard of living *never* before known to mankind.

"After American farmers have fed everyone in the United States, they export 60 percent of their wheat and rice to the rest of the world. They also produce more than half the entire world's wheat crop. American farmers have achieved this stupendous feat even though since 1940 the number of farms and farm workers has decreased by two thirds. In fact, despite fewer farms and farmers, America's agricultural output during that time has increased by 75 percent."

Although the message is from one of Richard's earlier speeches, only the numbers have changed. Our faith in America has never wavered. When he spoke, my eyes filled with tears. I felt proud—proud of my son and proud to be an American. And I think everyone in the 7,500-seat, capacity-filled Dallas Convention Center shared that pride. America offers such unlimited opportunity.

This speech was only one of hundreds delivered to Mary Kay audiences that have contained strong overtones of patriotism. I know in some circles it's not considered good taste to wave the flag at company gatherings. I disagree. We think it's a healthy emotion, and a message that can never be told too often.

In all the markets where Mary Kay does business, we seek
to instill deep pride in the culture and traditions of
Mary Kay, as well as that of each nation. It's often
remarked that Mary Kay's message is not only timeless,
but also universal in appeal, as it easily crosses language,
cultural, and geographic barriers.

The American Dream Comes True

I strongly believe in the American Dream. Mary Kay is living
proof that it can happen. Only in America could my story have
been possible. In 1963 when the company opened its doors, I
refused to listen to those negative people who were predicting
failure. My accountant told me there were "not enough cents in
the dollar" for the commission schedule we were proposing. My
attorney wrote to Washington for a list of all cosmetics companies
that had gone bankrupt that year. During our second month in
business, a California cosmetics manufacturer made me an offer:
"Mary Kay, I'll pay you a token amount for your formulas,
because you're *never* going to make it." Other financial "experts"
insisted we couldn't run a direct sales company without extending
a line of credit to the independent sales force.

The soothsayers prophesied that I was doomed to failure.
However, I was determined to prove them wrong. The odds were
against me, and I'll readily admit there were many things I didn't
know, but I *did* know four things for certain:

- People will support that which they help to create.
- In this great country there is *no limit* to what an individual can
  accomplish.

- If given the opportunity, women are capable of superior performance.

- I was willing to work long, hard hours to implement my convictions.

The annals of American business are filled with "impossible dreams" that have come true. I believed in those dreams, and most importantly, I believed in *my* dream.

Throughout the years, I have told my story to hundreds of thousands of women. I have always believed it is good for them to know that if a retired woman with grandchildren can establish a successful business, so can they. I have always regarded the independent sales force as a microcosm of the American free enterprise system. Regardless of age, gender, religion, race, education, or work experience, everyone who joins Mary Kay as a Beauty Consultant enters the business on an equal footing with other Beauty Consultants. She literally becomes president of her own company. We assist her by offering the tools that can help her succeed. In the true free enterprise spirit, each woman gets out of her business that which she is willing to put in. She is her own boss, and no one tells her when or whether to work. If she is a self-starter and if she relies upon the expertise available to her, she can rapidly build a successful business.

There are millions of people in the direct-selling industry, and the majority of them are women. I think that this dispels any myth that women are afraid to venture into business. Entrepreneurial in every sense of the word, these women are risk-takers and have demonstrated their capacity to be self-motivating. As I write this, women in the United States own more than half of the nation's assets. In contrast, women throughout the rest of the world own only one-tenth of the assets. At present, two-thirds of the world's other women are illiterate.

During her lifetime, Mary Kay Ash was able to fulfill her
dream to offer a business ownership opportunity to women
throughout the world. Currently, Mary Kay® products are
sold in more than 35 markets worldwide. Many of those
same underserved and underemployed women she wrote
about in this book have learned about free enterprise and
entrepreneurship with the Mary Kay opportunity in their
own countries. From Asia to Europe to North and South
America, women share similar basic goals—to better themselves and their families.

In some countries women are so oppressed that they may be
arrested for revealing their faces in public! Needless to say, by comparison, women in this country have tremendous opportunities.

It's popular in some circles to dwell upon what's wrong with
America. Certainly we are not a nation without faults, but I believe
there is a need today for us all to counter negativism by emphasizing
what's *right* with America. Skeptics tell me I was lucky to have started
my business when I did, claiming it's now more difficult to achieve
success. I think the opposite is true—there are more opportunities
today, especially for women, than at any other time in history. More
opportunities also have opened up for everyone in new fields of
education, technology, and the arts. People complain, "Things aren't
what they were in 'the good old days.'" I remember when the
1950s were "the good old days." Ten years from now, these current
days will be "the good old days!" Opportunities *have* always and *will*
always be around. You simply have to take advantage of them.

Make Opportunities Happen

Now and then, I'll hear a retired person who's having trouble
making ends meet: "You know, in all my life I've never had a
lucky break. If I had only had an opportunity, I could have done
something and been somebody."

I find this hard to accept. I believe everyone in America has count-less opportunities. But you cannot sit and wait for those opportunities to come knocking at your door. You have to *make* things happen. It's unfortunate when capable people in our great land of opportunity aren't willing to exert themselves enough to go after what's out there waiting for them. Our nation offers so much to so many.

If I sound as though I'm doing a little flag-waving, well, I am. I consider myself blessed to be an American. I also believe every leader who shares this strong emotion of patriotism should stand up and announce it to the world. Don't be shy about letting others know how you feel. It's good for your people to hear you speak up for what's right about America. It's good for your com-pany. And most important, it's good for America!

I also believe every successful leader has an obligation to be a good "corporate citizen." If you hold a responsible position in your company, you should make a major commitment to the cultural, educational, and philanthropic institutions of your community. Not only will those activities broaden your horizons through a healthy exchange of ideas with other business leaders in your area, but your efforts will also serve as a good role model for others. The best way to pay your dues to your country is to help build a better place in which we all may live.

Through the years, Mary Kay Inc. has continued to act upon this profound and timeless message that was one of the cornerstones of our founding. Giving back is a hallmark of the Mary Kay culture, the Company, and the Mary Kay Ash Charitable Foundation, which our Founder established to extend outreach across the United States to causes closely aligned with our mission. Mary Kay subsidiaries around the globe have followed this lead through philanthropic efforts in their own markets.

Independent National Sales Directors Talk about
Mary Kay Principles in Action Today

"During the process of building my business, I can remember the 110 percent I gave toward helping others reach their goals. Giving my time, energy, and expertise like Mary Kay always advocated really paid off. What happened? They wanted us to succeed as much for themselves as they did for the whole area. Each individual experienced being part of something bigger than themselves. They felt such pride to be affiliated with what we were becoming," says **Lise Clark** of the United States, a former Miss New Mexico who learned firsthand, "How you lead is what is passed down to everyone you come in contact with."

Ke Tang of China sees pride as a way to "Express our gratitude to life."

During one of the most difficult periods of her personal life, **Graciela Ardiles** of Argentina recalls, "My smile, my strength, my temperance were put to the test of my life. I felt my responsibility as a leader was to teach by example. Mary Kay taught me that because of what I had been through with my husband leaving me, I could help other women be strong, believe in themselves, enjoy their independence, and achieve economic autonomy. Today, when I hear my children speak with pride of their mother and what I have built, I know that from this book came my strength."

15 You Can't Rest on Your Laurels

In Lewis Carroll's *Alice's Adventures in Wonderland*, the Red Queen advises Alice: "Now, here you see, it takes all the running you can do to keep in the same place. If you want to get somewhere else, you must run twice as fast!"

Although Carroll wasn't thinking of today's business world, his advice is nonetheless applicable. It takes "all the running you can do" to become a leader, but you must "run twice as fast" to progress. At Mary Kay Inc. we express the thought in this way: "You can't rest on your laurels; for nothing wilts faster than a laurel rested upon."

In a career you either go forward or backward, but you don't stand still. Every one must continually improve his or her skills in a lifetime self-improvement program.

As you are planning such a program, I think it's good to remember the following guidelines:

- Embrace change,
- Become thoroughly knowledgeable in every aspect of your business,
- Don't forget the basic skills that got you started,
- Keep yourself in perspective by never getting "too big for your job,"

- Share your ideas with others; it helps both you and the idea
  grow stronger.

Like all businesses, the cosmetics field is ever changing. New
challenges are constantly brought about by transitions in lifestyles,
technology, and social events. We are committed to a continuous
search for new ideas and methods to improve our product line,
always striving to be the world leader in beauty and skin care. This
search for excellence demands an ongoing, all-out effort by our
leadership team. Everyone must keep abreast of developments in
his or her areas of expertise.

At the very least, a leader must strive to maintain the level of
his or her company's rate of growth. If your company, for
example, has a 25 percent annual growth rate, you should ask
yourself, "Did my performance grow by 25 percent in the past
year?" If the answer is no, your question should be, "What can
I do to increase that growth?" And don't forget, when inflation
is taken into consideration, a no-increase year represents negative
growth.

Know Your Business Thoroughly

We want the independent sales force to be experts in skin care. A
truly professional person must *know* her business thoroughly from
every angle. After all, today's women are better informed in all
facets of their lives. And this includes the subject of skin care. If an
Independent Beauty Consultant isn't thoroughly prepared for her
skin care classes, her "students" may be more knowledgeable than
she! Beauty Consultants gain this expertise through self-instructional
materials, classroom study, and firsthand experience.

In the beginning, a new Beauty Consultant should assume
that we know more about the cosmetics business than she does.

Thus, she should consider following her Independent Sales Director's instructions to the letter. After all, the Company and her Sales Director are in her corner, rooting for her. Over the years, we've developed tools for success that have worked for thousands. You wouldn't expect a student to study algebra without first learning basic mathematics. The same logic applies in our business and every business: You must master the basics before you can proceed. But progress cannot mean an abandonment of the basics. Too many people find themselves in trouble when they stray from the basics that were responsible for their earlier success! Time and again, I've seen both salespeople and leaders start off brilliantly only to falter somewhere down the road. Why? Because they didn't stick to the basics.

Once, I received a call from a member of the sales force who was on the verge of quitting. "Mary Kay, I was doing a record job during my first three months in the business, but my last several skin care classes have produced very few results, and I can't seem to book more." I'd heard this many times before, so I knew what questions to ask. After a few minutes of conversation, I learned she had stopped doing all the things that had worked so well for her when she was a new Beauty Consultant.

"No, I don't say that anymore," she answered when I asked if she was using our standard materials. She then told me how she had modified almost every technique she had originally learned. "It just doesn't sound like me, Mary Kay," she would repeat each time I questioned her.

"It's worked for so many other people," I pointed out to her, "and it worked for *you* when you used it." I asked that she promise to try it our way once more and call me the following week. When I talked to her again, she was happy to announce that she had turned everything around. "I've learned my lesson, Mary Kay, and you know, it even sounds like *me* now!" This woman went on to become an outstanding Independent Sales Director.

Like other leading companies, we have a time-tested formula for developing successful Mary Kay Independent Beauty Consultants that works if followed. But we also suggest extending oneself even further. In any work, the easiest way to begin is by learning all you can about your business. Read your company newsletters and magazines. Get out your basic manual and reread it. I think you'll be surprised how much information is there and how much you may have forgotten or missed the first time around. Time spent driving can also be a good opportunity to listen to instructional and motivational tools. I also recommend attending seminars and conferences, thus having the chance to hear and meet successful people in your field as they share their stories. You'll be surprised how willing experts are to share their success stories. It makes them feel important; successful people, like everybody else, wear the *invisible sign—Make me feel important.* I believe successful people in every field subscribe to a lifetime self-improvement program. Prominent doctors spend hours each week reading medical journals; attorneys read law journals; teachers, education materials; and CPAs, current tax revisions. Leading professionals in all fields attend seminars regularly. Once success is achieved, a person cannot rest on his laurels. He or she must move forward. A champion boxer knows he can't take it easy after winning a title bout. Actors cannot rely on past successes to keep them in the limelight. Once you've reached the top, you've got to work harder than ever to stay there.

I know the founder of an insurance company who became extremely wealthy, but his success went to his head. He stopped growing, his thinking became outdated, and his company was no longer innovative—the very quality that had made it successful.

Today the company has lost its position as an industry leader because its CEO became obsolete.

A former comptroller of a large corporation once came to us for a job. During the interview we learned that although he had enjoyed a successful career in his younger days, he had built his department to a point where he delegated *everything*. It was fine for him to delegate responsibility to other people, but he failed to grow with them. He didn't keep abreast of changes in his field. When his company computerized its operations, he never bothered to learn anything about the new technology and how it would improve efficiency. Eventually, the people working under him became computer experts, while he remained so far removed from their work that he didn't even understand what they were doing. The position overwhelmed him; his job went beyond him. In the end, he was so useless that his salary could no longer be justified. By failing to keep abreast of major changes in his field, he, too, became obsolete.

Sales Directors are cautioned about "executivitis." Sometimes a Beauty Consultant will work very hard to become a Sales Director, and then, having achieved that goal, she begins to "play executive." She no longer conducts skin care classes and eases up on her recruiting efforts. She stops doing the very things that earned her success and won her advancement to the position of Independent Sales Director!

Learn from the Successes of Others

At Mary Kay Inc. we conduct many conferences and Seminars for the independent sales force. These meetings are highly motivational and very informative. In addition to the scheduled format, these gatherings provide an excellent opportunity for women to exchange ideas. In the past, we invited nationally known and prominent professional speakers to address our large regional and national meetings, but now we encourage our own people to speak. While professional speakers were able to motivate Beauty Consultants for the moment, they didn't offer the kind of practical information tailored to their businesses. The top sales force achievers provide specifics that every person in the audience can apply. And since speakers must be star performers in order to speak, they serve as excellent role models. Their comments are immediately identifiable because they—just like everyone else in the audience—began as Beauty Consultants. When a woman hears the speaker's success story, she usually asks herself, "What has she got that I can't have fixed?"

Share Valid Ideas with Others

A strong sense of sharing prevails throughout the independent sales force and the Company; anyone who has a valid idea is encouraged to share it. My theory has always been if I have an idea and you have an idea—and I give mine to you and you give yours to me—then we each have two! But if I keep mine and you keep yours, we each still have only one apiece. Free exchange provides an ideal climate for learning and growing. Everyone is encouraged to exert herself in order to improve her performance. As Woodrow Wilson said, "I use not only all the brains I have, but all that I can borrow."

We encourage *all* our people to grow, not just those in sales. Our corporate staff attends conferences and seminars in their areas of specialization, and we foster further education and enrichment programs for all employees. Through our continuing education program the Company pays tuition for employees for college-level courses taken in one's field of specialization.

I believe many women take advantage of such educational programs because current management opportunities were previously not available to women. In some ways, there's still catching up to do, and many believe that in order to compete with men they must give a 110 percent effort. Our doors have always been wide open for the advancement of women, even when other companies were just beginning to consider women for top positions. I'm glad so many women have responded to opportunities for self-improvement.

None of us can afford to rest on our laurels. And that includes me. In 1963 I survived what I now call my "resting-on-my-laurels month." It was that brief period during which I considered retirement. I lived across from a funeral home at the time, and I almost called them to come and get me! You know the rest of the Mary Kay story: I decided to implement my life-long dream.

And I'm not finished yet! Recently my son Richard led an executive conference on the subject of retirement. The officers of our Company rationally debated the pros and cons of a 65, 75, or unlimited retirement age. I found myself sinking lower and lower in my chair. As we left the meeting, I said to Richard, "You know, you were talking about your mother in there."

He stopped and turned to me with astonishment.

"Why, Mom, it never occurred to me that *you'd* retire. I honestly never think of you as getting old!"

Right there in the office corridor I put my arms around him and kissed him!

I *still* have a career goal: I'll continue working as *hard* as ever so that every single day I can watch just one more woman reach her full potential and realize how great she really is!

Mary Kay Ash assumed the title of Chairman Emeritus in 1987. She remained active in the business until suffering a stroke in 1996. She maintained a steady interest and involvement with the independent sales force and staff until her death on Thanksgiving Day in 2001.

Independent National Sales Directors Talk about Mary Kay Principles in Action Today

"All of us tend to stay on course, but with the Mary Kay marketing plan, we literally wipe the slate clean every Seminar. Hearing our Founder talk about that, and then reading it in this book, I have been so encouraged to consistently set new goals. Because of that, I've experienced so much growth," said **Renee Hackleman** of the United States.

"With five major moves in my career," says **Pat Fortenberry**, wife of a United States Air Force officer, "I was always starting over. Each time I moved, people didn't realize my accomplishments. So I had to go back to the basics and back to building my team personally."

"We should never stop having goals. Mary Kay believed that before reaching one, we should already be thinking of the next one," said **Leticia Moguel Paz** of Mexico.

16 Be a Risk-Taker

When we started our business, we were well aware of the risks. Every single penny I had went into the investment. My son Richard, a life insurance agent, quit his $480-a-month job to work with his mother on her "crazy" idea at $250 a month. A few months later, my son Ben gave up a $750-a-month job in Houston and moved his family to Dallas to join us—for the same pay as his younger brother!

Richard and Ben took substantial reductions in salary, and my lifetime savings of $5,000 was on the line. I desperately wanted to start my own business; it was my only chance to be self-employed. All bridges were burned behind us. The business had to succeed. If I failed, as a middle-aged woman in the early 1960s, it would have been very difficult for me to find a job.

Unquestionably, being at risk was the major inspiration for also being innovative, hardworking, and highly motivated. Thank goodness America's free enterprise system was alive and well. Our hard work paid off, and we were rewarded for our efforts. At Mary Kay Inc. we encourage people to display the same kind of "risk-taking" spirit that inspired us in our early days. There's a certain type of person who thrives in such an environment—particularly when adequate incentives are provided—and I feel that it's the job of leaders to create this atmosphere.

People Fail Forward to Success

A risk-taking environment starts at the top of a corporation. If the
CEO doesn't have this spirit, chances are you won't find it anywhere else in the organization. It's a quality that permeates from
above; the CEO gives executive officers freedom to take risks, and
they in turn extend the same freedom to those who report to
them. Each leader, within his area of responsibility, is a decision-
maker. And when two leaders are in conflict, top management
supports the person under whose jurisdiction the decision
belongs.

Of course, there are times when decisions are made that
ultimately prove to be incorrect. This is bound to happen in a
company that encourages its people to take risks. At Mary Kay
Inc. we have a popular saying that is most applicable: "People fail
forward to success." I think it's vital for people to be free to take
risks and to be permitted mistakes along the way. This is what
nourishes personal growth and creativity.

I failed miserably at my very first Mary Kay skin care class. I
was anxious to prove that our skin care products could be sold to
small groups of women, and I wanted to make my first show a
huge success. But that evening I sold a grand total of $1.50. When
I left, I drove around the corner, put my head on the steering
wheel, and cried. "What's wrong with those people?" I asked
myself. "Why didn't they buy this fantastic product?" Bursts of
fear flashed through my mind. My initial reaction was to doubt
my new business venture. I became worried because my lifetime
savings were tied up in this Company. I looked in the mirror and
asked myself, "What did *you* do wrong, Mary Kay?" Then it hit
me: I had never even bothered to ask anyone for an order. I had
forgotten to pass out order cards and had just expected those
women to buy automatically! You can bet I didn't make the same
mistake at the next skin care class.

Yes, I failed—and for a few brief moments, I was fearful. But after analyzing what had happened, I *learned* from that failure. I've shared this story thousands of times with our Mary Kay audiences. I want them to know that I failed at my first skin care class, but refused to give up. I failed forward to success. I truly believe that life is a series of many attempts and many failures before we realize success. The important thing is to keep on trying.

Even before that fateful skin care class, I had known failure. Years earlier, my first job was with a company that sold its products through the party plan, and during my first few weeks, I averaged only $7 a party! The hostess received a $5 gift, and with a $7 sales volume, you can easily see that I had a problem! But I constantly looked for ways to improve my skills, and eventually I became a top salesperson.

Today, I like to remind people that it wasn't easy for me either when I started out. But there's no disgrace in failing. The only true failure is the person who gives up. Someone once remarked to Thomas Edison that he failed 25,000 times while experimenting with the storage battery. "No, I didn't fail," the brilliant inventor replied, "I discovered 24,999 ways that the storage battery doesn't work." In his lifetime, Edison received 1,093 patents for inventing such devices as the phonograph, motion pictures, the electric pen, waxed paper, and, of course, the incandescent lamp. Imagine the number of times Edison experienced failure during his long, re-markable career. We can all be thankful for his tenacity in refusing to accept a single failure as a permanent defeat.

While it's true that there's risk associated with starting any new business, and since there's no way of knowing in advance who has the intestinal fortitude to succeed in our field, I simply believe that every woman should be given the opportunity to consider starting her own Mary Kay business. If she succeeds, it could be the best opportunity she ever had. Yes, it's a calculated risk, but a woman can greatly improve the odds by applying hard work and tenacity. When a new Independent Beauty Consultant decides to start her business, she makes a small investment in a Starter Kit, which gives her the essentials to hold her first skin care classes. Should she also place an inventory order, we minimize this risk by guaranteeing to buy back any unused product at 90 percent of her cost within one year after the date it was purchased. Some start their businesses on a part-time basis until they're convinced they will enjoy it and make a good living as an Independent Beauty Consultant. Someone with another full-time position, for example, can start by conducting skin care classes in the evenings and on weekends. Thus, she would terminate her original job only after she had proved to herself that she could earn enough money in her Mary Kay business to warrant a full-time commitment. In this way, she reduces the risk inherent in a straight commission selling position.

Not Every Idea Will Be a Winner

When any company encourages innovation, it must accept the fact that not every acceptable idea will be a winner. In fact, a creative new project that arouses everyone's excitement when it is presented may be very disappointing after it is tried out. Several years ago, for example, we had such a project called "Business in a Box." This was a system to assist the independent sales force with organizing their bookkeeping and managing their time. It was the brainchild of one of our vice presidents, and once the idea was approved, we incurred considerable expense in setting it up. While its main purpose was to simplify bookkeeping, the independent sales force thought it was overly complicated, and they roundly rejected it. We ended up with a warehouse full of boxes that had absolutely no value to anyone outside the Mary Kay organization. The project failed, but its creator was not ostracized for that. To have done so would have discouraged others from submitting *their* creative ideas.

Independent National Sales Directors Talk about Mary Kay Principles in Action Today

"The biggest risk is failure. People fear failure as something which is very embarrassing. Mary Kay seemed to be telling us that more disappointing than failing, is to never try," says **Lisa Madson** of the United States.

"One must run risks in attempting success," says Lilia Lozano de Cuevas of Mexico, who discovered in this book the "greatness of Mary Kay's leadership."

"It always feels risky when a person is doing something different for the first time. To advance in any business involves learning to initiate new skills and moving out of comfort zones. Mary Kay was very good at getting us to see this," says **Idell Moffett** of the United States.

17 Work and Enjoy It

I once knew a 26-year-old businessman who always kept himself in top physical condition. At the office, however, he seemed to merely go through the motions, never really putting in a full day's work. By 4 P.M., he could barely keep his eyes open. Dragging himself into the house, he'd tell his wife, "I'm bushed, honey. Don't make any plans for tonight; I'm going to bed early." But let one of the boys call for a racquetball game, and suddenly he'd snap awake, ready for hours of strenuous activity on the court.

I also once knew a wealthy 85-year-old real estate developer who put in a solid 10-hour workday every day. At any time, he had many projects underway. He thrived on his work and was an inspiration to everyone who knew him. Everyone marveled at his apparently inexhaustible energy. "Where does he get it?" people asked. "I hope I have that much energy when I'm his age." The fact is most people don't have that much energy at half his age!

The More People Enjoy Their Work, the More Energy They Give It

It's a disturbing paradox to compare that physically fit young person, who lacked the energy to work a full day at the office, with this youthful octogenarian who could outwork all of us! Obviously, the difference is one of attitude. In my experience, the more people enjoy their work, the more energy they have to put into it! Furthermore, we generally perform or work *better* if we enjoy it.

Recently, I had the following conversation with a young schoolgirl:

"How's everything going in school?"

"Okay, I guess."

"How are you doing in history?" I asked, trying to be a little more specific.

"Terrible. It's so boring. I fall asleep in class every day."

"And how about English?"

"Same thing. I'm failing. I can't keep my eyes open there either. We really have a terrible teacher."

"And science?"

"Oh," she suddenly brightened and her eyes lit up, "I'm getting an A in science. I just love it, especially the lab work. I think I'm going to be a scientist when I grow up. I can't wait to go on our field trip next week."

I didn't have to be told the subjects in which she was doing poorly and the one in which she was excelling. The correlation between good grades and her enjoyment of the subject was obvious. I can remember how much I always enjoyed English and that I always got straight A's in that subject. When adults are questioned about their work, similar likes and dislikes are revealed, which correlate directly to their performances. For example:

"I'm having trouble with my approach to new prospects," a salesperson will say.

"What seems to be the problem?"

"I don't know exactly. Maybe it's because I don't feel comfortable meeting new people. Once I get my foot in the door, however, I give a good presentation and sell to practically everyone."

"Any ideas why that happens?" I ask.

"Well, the part I enjoy most about selling is getting to know people and helping them solve their problems."

No matter what a person's occupation, you'll hear the same message. A secretary who can't quite master her word processor: "I'm not mechanically inclined, and I just don't like computers." The owner of a small retail store: "I can't stand detail work. I never was any good at bookkeeping." A self-employed accountant: "The least appealing part of my work is having to join a lot of civic and charitable organizations in order to drum up new clients." Even a writer: "It's the research that gets me down."

Let's face it, all of us have to do some unpleasant tasks in our work. But if they have to be done, we do them. I cope by putting the most unpleasant tasks at the top of my list of things that must be done each day. Once they are out of the way, the rest of the day goes much more smoothly. To make things a little more interesting, I make a game out of the most tedious jobs. With housekeeping chores, for example, I might compete against myself to see how fast I can finish a given job. When I ironed shirts as a young housewife years ago, I had it down to two and a half minutes per shirt! Today I still play "beat the clock" while doing dictation work that I've taken home from the office. My attitude has always been to make the best of whatever work you have to do and enjoy it.

People have said that I'm a "born salesperson" because I enjoy selling so much, and I'm sure that this enjoyment was the prime reason for my early successes. I've worked with other salespeople who I thought had more talent, but I outsold them because I made more calls than they did. To them, selling was drudgery.

To me, it was a game. I got a special thrill from the challenge of booking shows for the household products company I represented. Most of the women who attended those parties came because they felt obligated to the hostess, who was either a close friend or a relative. Few women wanted to spend hours listening to a salesperson extol the virtues of floor wax, furniture polish, or toilet bowl cleaner. But for me, that's where the challenge was: getting those women so excited about my products that they *enthusiastically* gave me their orders.

A Good Product, an Interested Audience, the Unknown

Mary Kay Independent Beauty Consultants are more fortunate because they have a glamorous product to present. Women today are genuinely interested in skin care. And there is a third factor in selling that is always fascinating: the *unknown*. Every skin care class is different; you never know in advance exactly what circumstances you may encounter. To me this element of surprise has always been exciting. For some salespeople, however, it sets off a completely different reaction—arousing feelings of insecurity and self-doubt.

There's no question that people perform better doing work they enjoy. Every leader should therefore strive to create an atmosphere in which his people can enjoy their work. If people must work under great pressure, merely piping in music won't improve the situation *or* their performance. But if you are at least aware that a problem exists, you have taken a step in the right direction. There may not be much you can do to change people's basic aptitudes, but you can often improve their working environment by reducing stressful conditions. One way to do this is to create an atmosphere that allows your people to feel free and uninhibited. I remember how much stress I suffered under a former leader who stood guard over the office like a watchman. He intimidated us all to the point that we were afraid to look up from our work. We felt like prisoners. His fear tactics were counterproductive, however, because people can't give their best performances under highly stressful conditions. As a result, the entire staff was error prone, absenteeism and personnel turnover were unusually high, and company loyalty was totally lacking. Everyone had but a single purpose for showing up at work: to get a paycheck. Our supervisor made it clear that he didn't care how we felt or what we thought! And, we responded in kind to him and the company. Some of the people, I think, felt so bitter toward the company that they secretly hoped it would fail! We felt miserable, and our low productivity showed it. It was the lack of personal freedom that crippled us, and the company unfortunately paid dearly for it.

I've painted a very dreary picture of what happens to people who are unhappy in their work. You may think it's exaggerated, but I assure you that it is not. People do not respond positively to leaders who browbeat them. However, they do respond to praise. Good people leaders bestow praise when their people succeed, no matter how small that success might be. We all need recognition. These feelings enhance self-esteem and reinforce self-confidence, and the result is reflected in a higher quality of work.

A Good Leader Tries to Match the Person to the Appropriate Job

Sometimes a person performs poorly at his job because he's doing the wrong kind of work for him. One morning after spending several long hours with my personal CPA, I commented, "I don't know how you do this. I could never work with all those numbers and tax rulings for 10 hours a day, as you do. I would find it painfully tedious."

"Mary Kay, I could never go out and sell like you do," he replied. "I don't know how you're able to get out of bed every day to make those calls. Frankly, your kind of work would be much more difficult for me."

Isn't it wonderful that we're all different? If we all liked the same things and did the same things, what a dull world it would be. His frankness reminded me of this basic truth that we should never forget: We are all different. A good leader will recognize those differences and treat each person as an individual. A good leader will also detect when someone lacks the aptitude needed for a particular job, and she will try her best to find a more appropriate assignment. At Mary Kay Inc. we have frequently reassigned good, loyal people to positions for which their talents were better suited. Once relocated, their levels of performance often increased dramatically. Why? Because they were enjoying their new positions. To state the obvious once again: People do their best work when they're happy!

Enthusiasm Is Contagious, But So Is Negativism

Leaders sometimes say to me, "Yes, I want my people to be happy and enjoy their work. But how do you suggest I achieve this?" The way to begin is by taking a self-inventory. I suggest that they ask themselves, "Am I happy with my work?" "Do I enjoy it?" "Does my job excite me?" As I said in an earlier chapter, enthusiasm is contagious. But there's a reverse side to that coin: Negativism is also contagious. If a leader comes to work grouchy or depressed, his mood is bound to affect those around him, and they, in turn, are likely to pass it along. The happiest people I have known are those who eagerly look forward to beginning work each morning. I firmly believe that most successful people feel that way about their work. Their vocations are like avocations. Dr. Joyce Brothers once said that being a workaholic isn't all bad; it just means total commitment to work that you enjoy.

Dr. Denton Cooley, the world-famous heart surgeon who performed countless open-heart operations, once confessed to being addicted to work. "I am most relaxed and have the most mental peace when I'm working," he said. "One characteristic of an addict is that he has withdrawal symptoms when he's unable to indulge his addiction. I feel the same way when I'm not at my work. This is particularly true when I go on vacation. I feel uneasy—almost frantic—to get back on the job." Early in his career, he worried about being too confined and thought that perhaps he should spend a few afternoons on the golf course. So after he tried golf, he reported the result: "I have completely accepted my work as my 'hobby.' Some men get their enjoyment on the golf course. I get mine from practicing my specialty." No wonder Dr. Cooley has been recognized as one of the world's greatest surgeons.

I, too, derive my keenest enjoyment from my work. And because I feel this way, I often work in preference to indulging in what others might call "fun." My work is fun, and I feel very fortunate to be able to derive so much pleasure from it.

Independent National Sales Directors Talk about Mary Kay Principles in Action Today

"People very much need to know and feel that they and what they do are important. Women in particular need the ability to work with flexibility and without tension. This chapter is so poignant today because people are tense. I tell them to love their work, to enjoy it. If you do this right, I tell them, you're going to have a good life," says **Maribel Barajas** of the United States.

"Mary Kay taught me to enjoy and be proud of our profession. She wanted all of us to find a need and fill it. We were building relationships in the process. That's exactly how this great organization has produced so many successful independent businesswomen," says **Jeanne Curtis** of the United States.

For **Gerri Nicholson** of the United States, it was a simple matter of taking ownership of the dream Mary Kay always emphasized. "Love the product so much until you feel that everyone would benefit and should be wearing it! Once you're sold, then you can see that the sky is within your reach."

"Women want to live up to expectations; they want to succeed. Many come from such non-praising environments that this kind of message is like a breath of fresh air! People need excitement; they love to be around others who enjoy what they're doing," says **Pam Ross** of the United States, a former college athlete whose former boss once told her she wasn't cute enough to sell makeup.

18 Nothing Happens Until Somebody Sells Something!

During our second year in business, I wanted to impress upon our Company employees the importance of the independent sales force and to emphasize that if these independent sales force members were not out there selling our products, we would cease to exist. So I sent them the following memorandum:

A CONSULTANT OR DIRECTOR is the most important person in our business—she is our ONLY customer!

A CONSULTANT OR DIRECTOR is dependent upon us—and we are dependent upon *her*.

A CONSULTANT OR DIRECTOR is not an interruption of our work—she is the *purpose* of it.

A CONSULTANT OR DIRECTOR does us a favor when she calls—we are not doing her a favor by serving her.

A CONSULTANT OR DIRECTOR is a part of our business—not an outsider.

A CONSULTANT OR DIRECTOR is not a cold statistic—she is a flesh-and-blood human being with feelings and emotions just like our own.

A CONSULTANT OR DIRECTOR is not someone with whom to argue or match wits.

A CONSULTANT OR DIRECTOR is a person who brings us her needs—it is our job to fill those needs.

A CONSULTANT OR DIRECTOR is deserving of the most courteous and attentive treatment we can give.

A CONSULTANT OR DIRECTOR is the *lifeblood* of this business!

We would appreciate your cooperation in daily acknowledging each and every one of these points. Why not keep this card on your desk as a reminder of how important each Consultant and Director is to us.

This last paragraph was added several years later, and the entire memo was printed on four-by-six-inch pink cards, which I still distribute when I visit our branch offices. I hand the card to people and explain: "I realize there are times when Beauty Consultants or Sales Directors come to you with complaints that you may think are unreasonable. When this happens, I'd like you to remember that if it weren't for them, we wouldn't have our jobs."

With hundreds of thousands of Independent Beauty Consultants and Independent Sales Directors, someone will occasionally direct a few harsh words to whomever is sitting behind an office desk. I constantly remind our staff that they should respond with tact and diplomacy. "Treat her like a queen," I say. "Remember—without her we don't have a job. We must never forget that she's the reason for our business. If you conduct yourself in this professional manner, the chances are that she will relax and tell you the *real* source of her concern."

"I'd like to have one of those pink Cadillacs and some of those lavish prizes too," employees will sometimes say.

My reply is direct: "If it weren't for the sales volume that an Independent Sales Director produces to earn her Cadillac, you might not be standing here as an employee wishing it were yours. They represent the carrots that motivate independent sales force members. The more pink Cadillacs out there, the better for all of us." We remind our staff that they should never begrudge the money an Independent Sales Director earns. Mary Kay independent sales force members work on a straight commission and are paid on their volume of sales. When they earn a great deal of money, you can be sure that they've worked very hard. I've known companies that thought their salespeople were overpaid and began to figure out ways to reduce their income. Such companies invariably rue the day they decided to lower sales commissions. One of my greatest joys is to see independent sales force members earn a lot of money. It makes me very happy and proud.

The Entire Company Should Be Sales-Oriented

I think all Company employees need to know that their jobs depend upon the independent sales force. Our manufacturing people know, "If the independent sales force doesn't sell it, we don't have anything to manufacture." We all have an obligation to back up the independent sales force, and if we fail to do so, we're not doing our jobs. Not only do I constantly try to get this message across in our corporate office, but I work equally hard to communicate this attitude to the sales force as well.

When tens of thousands of Independent Beauty Consultants and Independent Sales Directors visit Dallas for our annual Seminars, we conduct an open house. We don't just take them on tours through our offices and manufacturing facilities so that they can observe people at work; we set up stations where procedures are explained and questions are answered. We also encourage the independent sales force to direct questions to employees at all levels of our organization. This kind of communication makes everyone feel that we're all on the same team, working together. It also builds mutual respect between employees and the independent sales force.

When both groups come to understand one another, a family-like atmosphere remains intact and the customer is better served. We want our staff to treat each Independent Beauty Consultant as an individual, not merely as a number in a huge and impersonal independent sales force. They must know that they're dealing with loving and caring people who depend on them. It does wonders for employee morale to discover firsthand how qualified and con-scientious the independent sales force is. And knowing that the Company's products are sold by salespeople of integrity is a source of considerable pride. I often say, "You're not just filling an order. You're helping someone who supports three children to make a living. If you make a mistake in her order or if she receives a defective product, you've created a serious problem for her, and I know that you would not want to do that."

It's also important for our staff to know that we must produce a superior product, so that people will come back for more. "Repeat business is all-important," I say, "and we must support the independent sales force so that their customers will order again and again."

Ideally, every employee in the Company should be sales-oriented. It doesn't matter if that person is in research, account-ing, or shipping—everyone's job supports the sales organization. Not a single major decision is made at Mary Kay Inc. without first weighing the consequences to the independent sales force.

In order for our staff to give their utmost support to the independent sales force, they must clearly understand what goes on in the field. To accomplish this, we make sure that every person in a leadership position has attended a training class on our marketing programs, skin care class procedures, and other independent sales force related activities. A person working in quality assurance or product design, for instance, will never fully grasp all the ramifications of his or her job without this face-to-face exposure to the customer. We also want everyone in our Company to be using Mary Kay® products daily. And as a way of encouraging this, we offer our products at a discount in limited quantities to employees.

We want to understand everything that is likely to happen in the field, so we keep in touch with the independent sales force. The more we know, the more we can help them grow their businesses. We encourage everyone to give us their suggestions, and we make every effort to provide a personal response. When something isn't working properly, we want to know about it—right away—so that it can be corrected.

The Company's Attitude Can Make or Break the Sales Force

I once was a part of a sales staff that was demoralized by negative attitudes of its management team. Once we attended a meeting where the president of the company addressed the entire sales organization. He took great pride in his staff people, but he obviously had little regard for his sales force. "We make the finest products of their kind in the world," he said. "We have the best people in our factories, and they work with the best machinery. Our shipping and warehousing departments are the envy of the industry." For 20 minutes he told us how wonderful the company was. It sounded good, but then he spoiled everything by adding, "It's you salespeople who constantly let us down. I don't think any one of you knows the first thing about selling. Our products are so good that if we had a trained dog to pass out brochures, it would outsell the best one of you." He made every salesperson in the room feel worthless. Evidently the company's staff people took their cue from the president. They talked down to the salespeople and acted as if they were doing us a favor to return a telephone call. We were treated like second-class citizens.

Even at company get-togethers, the staff people were aloof, gathering together in cliques. Their spouses behaved similarly, hardly ever exchanging social amenities with the salespeople. "It reminds me of how officers' wives treated lower-ranking officers' wives when my husband and I were stationed in Pensacola," a salesperson's wife remarked. "But that's the military, and I thought we were through with such treatment when we left the service." Eventually many of the spouses of the salespeople refused to attend company social gatherings. This negative attitude from within their own families became one more burden with which the sales force had to contend. It's difficult for anyone to have faith in his company and his own abilities when his spouse is unsupportive.

Build Self-Esteem and Confidence

A salesperson must have self-esteem and confidence to do well. And much of his or her attitude will depend upon the company's attitude toward its sales force. Let me illustrate my point with another example. Company A and Company B are competitors in the wholesale grocery business. Each company has salespeople who make daily calls selling and delivering pretzels, potato chips, and related products. However, there is a distinct difference in the attitude each company has toward its sales force. Company A insists that its salespeople wear uniforms, and it refers to them as *drivers*. Company B's salespeople wear sports jackets, work on a salary plus commission, and carry business cards that read *Account Representative*.

When a Company B salesperson comes into the office, the staff gives them the VIP treatment. As one salesman put it, "I haven't felt like such a hero since my high school football days. All of the office force knows who I am, and I'm constantly being asked to join a group for lunch. Everyone makes such a fuss over me—and I love it."

Unfortunately the salespeople at Company A have a very different story. The company lets them know in no uncertain terms that they're not welcome in the general offices. "The company has very plush offices, and I feel like an intruder when I come in," says one salesperson. "I just don't feel comfortable with those people; maybe it's this brown uniform I wear. I'm not treated like a productive member of a team." No wonder he feels that way. That's exactly how Company A feels about him and every other person in its sales force.

Needless to say, Company B attracts a much higher-quality salesperson, who out produces his counterpart at Company A three to one! Again, it all boils down to management's attitude toward its salespeople. And, positive or negative, management's attitude will be reflected in each salesperson's own self-image.

I am 100 percent committed to the independent sales force, placing each independent sales force member on a pedestal. "Well, that's because you have a sales background, Mary Kay," people will say. Yes, I identify with the independent sales force because that's where I came from, but not every manager with a selling background who has worked his or her way to the top thinks as I do. In fact, I recall one manufacturing executive who addressed his sales force with this: "I've been out there in the field just like every one of you in this room. And, believe me, I know every trick there is. If any of you think for one moment that you're going to pull the wool over my eyes, you're making a big mistake. There's nothing you can do that I haven't already done. So if you're thinking I don't trust salespeople, you're right, I don't. It takes one to know one, if you know what I mean!" Of course, this executive was a bad apple, and he assumed that every other salesperson was the same. This was not true, however, and every salesperson present in that room resented the presumption.

At a large manufacturing company's banquet, I once sat on the same dais with a CEO who delivered a truly wonderful message to his sales force. In part, he told them: "It's you salespeople gathered here tonight who are responsible for this company's record performance during the past year. It's true that our company's plant has the latest state-of-the-art facilities, and we've got an outstanding backup system to serve you. But we all know very well that nothing happens until somebody sells something." He then paused and wrote on a large blackboard in big, bold print: "Production minus sales equals scrap." He really meant it when he then said, "I'm proud to be associated with such fine men and women. I think you're the finest sales organization in the world."

Now, that's an inspiring message to deliver to *any* sales organization.

Independent National Sales Directors Talk about Mary Kay Principles in Action Today

"It's so important for leaders never to forget where they started and what caused their success. This chapter echoes that in order to teach with authenticity and integrity, leaders must step out of their comfort zones constantly if they expect others to follow their lead. Selling is the basis upon which all else rests," says **Kate DeBlander** of the United States.

"I always loved the advice Mary Kay Ash would give when someone wasn't doing well in her business," says **Janis Moon** of the United States. "She'd say we must get back to basics and to teaching women about beauty and skin care. It all starts from the beginning."

Even with a Harvard MBA, **Gloria Mayfield Banks** of the United States realized very quickly that the greatest opportunity for her was outside the traditional corporate world. After attending her first Mary Kay skin care class and seeing how easy the products were to sell, she recognized tremendous potential in the simple idea of "selling lipstick. People had a hard time believing we could build million dollar businesses from our kitchen table," she recalls, "yet so many of us have done just that."

"Just as Mary Kay said it would for those of us with an emphasis on selling the products, this selling focus becomes such a firm foundation – so much so that everything else in our business ripples off of it," says **Debi Moore** of the United States.

19 Never Hide behind Policy or Pomposity

Not long ago a friend's security alarm system broke down. The family was out of town, so the housekeeper called the security company to report the matter. "We'll send somebody out as soon as we have the owner's authorization to fix it," she was told. The housekeeper explained that the owner wouldn't return for a week, but the company insisted that without the owner's approval they would not repair it. In desperation the housekeeper asked me if I would call the company to see what I could do.

I called and was given the same answer.

"But they're not in town," I explained.

"I'm sorry, ma'am, but it's against company policy for us to fix it without their authorization," the man insisted.

"I understood that," I said patiently, "but what difference does it make? The housekeeper is in the house with the key, so she's obviously not a burglar. I suggest to you that, since you know she's not a burglar and the alarm is out of order, you repair it immediately. If you don't, a real burglar could break in, and your company might be held liable."

"What you say is very true, ma'am, and I agree with you. But it's against company policy . . . "

"May I speak to the manager?" I asked.

"Of course, but he'll tell you the same thing."

And he was right. "It's against company policy," the manager reiterated.

"But *why* do you have such a policy?" I asked.

"Well, we have lots of policies, ma'am, and I couldn't begin to explain the reasons for all of them. The home office in Chicago sets policy, and I just carry it out. I could get into a lot of trouble if I didn't."

Fortunately my salesmanship served me well, and I was able to convince the man to risk censure this one time and have the system repaired. But believe me, I was exasperated!

It's frustrating to be told only that "it's against company policy." But when you question the logic behind the policy and the manager or salesperson simply repeats, "It's against company policy," then you must assume that there is another reason for the refrain: That person *doesn't know* the answer.

The insecurity that accompanies this lack of knowledge causes him to hide behind an abstract villain—the company policy. He knows that if you are presented with this distant villain, your wrath toward him will diminish. Actually, it's a rather logical technique of self-preservation. It's easy to recognize this pattern in the behavior of others, but can you spot it in yourself? Have you ever been unable to explain—or defend—a company policy and turned to an inquisitive employee with "You can't, because it's against company policy"?

Don't State Company Policy without Giving the Reason for the Policy

I'm not suggesting that company policies be abolished. It's impossible to function without them. What I am suggesting is that you never state a company policy without explaining the reason behind it. Don't hide behind a policy! If you do, you'll alienate your people, as some companies do their customers. As frustrating as this mechanical response is to a customer, it's even more frustrating to an employee. If a customer doesn't like a company policy, he can take his business elsewhere. But terminating one's employment out of frustration is too extreme and costly a reaction. And so usually, an employee doesn't leave. He keeps his job, but his bitterness and resentment remain, thus undermining a healthy, positive employer-employee relationship.

At Mary Kay Inc., as at other companies, not every policy is well-received by everyone. If the policy exists, it exists for a good reason, and we abide by it. But we don't hide behind it!

Another policy that must exist because of the size of the Mary Kay independent sales force involves the transfer of an Independent Beauty Consultant from one unit to another. Very early in our history, personality clashes occurred, and Independent Beauty Consultants would request transfers to another Independent Sales Director's unit. We tried to monitor this kind of personality conflict, and in the beginning, we allowed transfers to be made. But it caused a great deal of friction among the Sales Directors. "Why did you let Betty leave my unit and join Susie's?" we'd hear. Consequently, we established a policy that permits an Independent Beauty Consultant to change units only after she has been completely inactive in her Mary Kay business for a full year, at which time she can restart her Mary Kay business under the

Sales Director of her choice, providing, of course, that she again qualifies for acceptance as an Independent Beauty Consultant.

Whenever possible, company guidelines and policies should be stated in writing so that there can be no misunderstanding of the company's position on pertinent issues. The more accessible this information is the more likely that disputes will be avoided. We believe in preempting potential problems by spelling everything out in advance. To accomplish this, we provide each Sales Director with a wide variety of educational tools and resources. I believe it is important to communicate clearly the foundations upon which our Company is built. We clearly communicate how commissions are earned at various sales levels for specific awards, recognitions, and promotions. With this basic information conveniently available to everyone, no charge of unfairness can be justified.

While it would be wonderful if everyone agreed with all company policies, it's not realistic to expect that. No company can please everyone all the time. But, provided they are given rational reasons, people do respect company policies that are fair. In fact, well-thought-out company policies often make people feel secure because they know in advance what to expect. Just imagine for a moment how frustrating it would be to work for a company that had no written policies.

With hundreds of thousands of independent representatives, we would have chaos without our excellent communication tools.

Many of the practices that companies observed back in the 1950s are illegal today—for example, the use of one policy for men and another for women. Other policies still practiced by some companies, however, are within the law, even though archaic. Such policies become entrenched in the system and are followed for years without being questioned. Some have roots that go back to the days before women were employed in the work force and were written *by* men and *for* men. One example would be the standardized 9-to-5 work day. This inflexible timetable has become a topic of much social concern as millions of working mothers struggle to find late-afternoon supervision for their school-age children. While policies such as this one may have made sense when they were written, they have long since been outdated. And in some giant industries, huge bureaucratic structures can delay changes in policy. I believe that women who are employed in such companies should voice their concerns. Frequently, a woman's insight offers a new point of view that had not been previously considered. When policies of this nature are challenged by women and sincere efforts are made to discuss them openly, positive changes can, and eventually will, result.

Every company is likely to have one or more policies that, in time, have become discriminatory or obsolete. Perhaps the best way for a leader to avoid implementing such policies is to make sure he or she never hides behind them. Don't just announce the policy, explain why: "This is company policy *because. . . .* " If you can't finish the sentence with a satisfactory reason, perhaps the time has come to modify or do away with the policy.

Obviously each company reviews current policies in a different manner. If an employee wished to initiate such a review, he or she should first learn the appropriate method, either from a supervisor or the personnel department. But whatever path is required—board action, peer review committee, or personnel management team—the employee must recognize that any change will require some basic strategies. These might include:

- Fully researching and documenting the rationale for the proposed change,
- Anticipating objections and preparing suitable answers,
- Identifying the person or persons within the organization who can lend powerful support to the change,

- Preparing for compromise or modified change,
- Constructing a policy to replace appropriately the one in question.

In other words, you can't just complain about an outdated policy—you must plan its replacement.

People may hide behind policy when they are insecure or uninformed or uncomfortable. But there's another, more destructive, condition: People can also hide behind pomposity.

Don't Let Success on the Corporate Ladder Go to Your Head

When people move up the corporate ladder, success sometimes goes to their heads. They trip over their own egos and lose those very qualities that earned them rapid advancement—the ability to work effectively with people and the ability to confront problems rationally and decisively. I've seen this unfortunate scenario repeated too many times. Eventually their pomposity causes them to slide right back down that ladder of success.

Why are so many otherwise talented people unable to handle success? Psychologists tell us that a person who "acts superior" is often covering up feelings of inferiority. And from my experience, I must agree. Successful people who feel secure about themselves—who they are, where their talents lie, what their limitations are—retain a sense of humility that enables them to view both the responsibilities of their positions and the demands on their time in balanced perspective. Those who can't handle success put on airs to cover up their inadequacies. Such artful camouflage, however, seldom conceals the truth.

It has been said that rich people are just poor people with money. The winner of a $5 million lottery is the same person the day after he wins—except that he's $5 million richer. The money will, of course, make a difference in his life. But if, as a result of his winnings, he becomes arrogant, overbearing, haughty, and self-important, he will lose the respect of others.

Success Depends on Total Team Effort

Every manager must realize that his success depends on a total team effort: people working together to reach the same objectives. Every person in an organization should have a sense of synchronization about his or her work. I emphasize this point to new employees during their orientation so that they will feel assured that their contributions to the company, however slight at the beginning, are nevertheless important. A person's title or the size of his paycheck does not determine my respect or regard for him. Every task is important, and when someone does it well, I make a special effort to express my appreciation. Whenever possible, I try to call everyone by name and pay him a compliment. For instance, if I happen to see the maintenance man I might say, "Bill, the office looks terrific, and you did a great job hanging all those pictures." Or if I don't see him, but I am aware of the good work he's done, I may leave a brief handwritten note: "Bill, I just want to let you know how much we appreciate the fine job you did fixing the air conditioner. It's much more comfortable now. Thanks. – Mary Kay." Unfortunately people who do behind-the-scenes maintenance work are too often overlooked. I've even seen maintenance personnel working in offices whose occupants ignored them, as if they were invisible. Well aware of this, I make a special effort to be cordial to them.

As the Company's Founder and chairman of the board, I feel that I should set a good example. So no matter whom the person may be—Company president or janitor—I make a sincere effort to let all Mary Kay people know they're very much appreciated. I've already told you there are no titles on the doors of any our corporate offices and that everyone is addressed by his or her first name. There are also no executive dining rooms at our corporate headquarters. Several years ago when our telephone system was being installed, I was asked if I needed a private number. I answered, "Heavens, no. No one will be calling me privately."

Don't Create an Atmosphere of "Haves" and "Have-Nots"

Believe me, it's not that I disapprove of executive dining rooms, executive bathrooms, or private phone lines in some offices. It's just that I do not wish to promote such superficial amenities within our Company. It's against our style to create an atmosphere that arouses hostile feelings between "haves" and "have-nots." This is what invariably happens when conspicuous status symbols are be-stowed upon a chosen few. I don't believe in promoting a privi-leged class. Such an environment breeds pomposity. And pomposity is demoralizing and self-defeating—as well as bad business.

I've seen many hard-working, unpretentious individuals climb rapidly into the executive suite only to rapidly become arrogant and overbearing. In my mind, there's no room in the executive suite for such people. In our organization such a turnabout leads to a predictable end: professional and personal embarrassment.

A Leader's Success Depends on the Ability to Develop and Motivate Others

We also emphasize that the independent sales force member who advances in her Mary Kay business should never forget that she, too, was once an Independent Beauty Consultant. As she

NEVER HIDE BEHIND POLICY OR POMPOSITY

advances, her success depends upon her ability to develop and motivate other women in her unit. An Independent Sales Director is most likely to succeed if her Independent Beauty Consultants can identify with her and ask themselves how they can be more like her. "What's she got that I can't have fixed?" is a popular Mary Kay expression often heard at our meetings. Most successful Sales Directors project the image of ordinary people who conscientiously do their work extraordinarily well. Her success is based upon the success of the women she mentors. Her attempt will backfire if she tries to convey to the women in her unit an image of superiority—by implication undermining their confidence and therefore their capacity to advance. Eventually such a person's high-handed manner, arrogance, and presumption—in short, her pomposity—will herald her downfall.

Unfortunately, some people are conditioned to look out only for themselves—even at the expense of others. Some managers are friendly with other managers, yet cold and aloof to those with less seniority. This haughty attitude can be found in every occupation in people who are defeated by success.

What can be done with such individuals? As I suggested earlier, people who hide behind pomposity usually do so out of fear and insecurity. And while I would never presume to give psychological or therapeutic advice to such an individual, my experience has provided me with a few hints that might be helpful to any leader.

First and foremost, I believe that you should look closely at your own thoughts and feelings. Are you insecure or hesitant in your role? If so, the answer is simply "Do your homework." As we discussed in Chapter 7, nothing removes insecurity like actual product knowledge and managerial experience.

Are you giving the appearance of pomposity? In other words, are you insensitive to the needs and feelings of others, thus giving them the impression that you are aloof and haughty? If so, I would suggest that you can reestablish yourself in the eyes of others by attending to the following guidelines:

- Always be truthful with your employees. If they ask for information you cannot reveal, say so. If they ask something that you don't know, say that as well. Most people are very quick to discern a smoke screen.

- Be consistent in facts and attitude. Not only will this help employees understand you, but it will also allow them to function with security.

- Be relaxed and confident when dealing with others. Even something as obvious as using a calm tone of voice can put your employees at ease. Think things through before you say them (be certain you are saying what you mean) and be yourself.

- Whenever possible, use "we" instead of "I" when discussing your team with others. Word will definitely get back that you accept and respect their contributions.

- Finally, always remember where you came from, and bear in mind that your future depends upon your ability to work well with people. While pomp is something that fascinates all of us on occasion, pomposity is never admirable—least of all in a leader.

Independent National Sales Directors Talk about Mary Kay Principles in Action Today

"The brilliance of this business is that no one is superior over the other. We all start the same. We're all connected in some manner, and because of this atmosphere, people have the courage to take more chances on themselves," says **Mattie Dozier** of the United States. "Mary Kay never wanted us to get so busy and self-important that the people looking to us for leadership begin to feel that they're not important enough for our time. It's never good to make people feel they're a little fish in a big pond. How can they possibly feel they can ever learn if that's the case?"

"Women naturally want to make a difference in others' lives. How genius," says **Mary Pat Raynor** of the United States, "that Mary Kay doesn't label a position with a specific earning capacity. Each individual decides exactly how much she wants to make, how much she is worth. What a heartwarming thing to succeed by putting dedication and love into other people's lives."

"People can always find a loophole for bad behavior or some attitude. I always teach that it's what you actually do that counts. *The Mary Kay Way* is, for me, the only way to do business," says **Ree Foster** of the United States.

20 Be a Problem-Solver

There's just no such thing as a problem-free business. And no matter what business you're in, most of the problems are people-related. Simply "surviving" or "weathering" these problems is not enough. You—as the leader—must take steps to resolve them. Such a problem-solving process takes a common pattern.

1. Recognition of the problem
2. Analysis of the problem
3. Definition of alternative solutions
4. Selection of the best alternative
5. Implementation
6. Follow-up and evaluation of results

The First Step in Problem Solving Is to Admit That a Problem Exists

The fact is that some people problems are more "real" than others. First you must allow for the chronic complainers. No matter how small the problem, they will embellish it. You will soon learn to identify these individuals in your organization. Don't ignore them, because every now and then they do have a legitimate complaint. Of course, you must know your business *and* your people well enough to be able to separate the real from the imaginary and the invented.

Productive people are usually so involved in their jobs they don't have time to complain. Nor do they allow trivial problems to interfere with their work. A good rule of thumb is to listen to every complaint but to pay closest attention to your most productive people.

With regard to leaders in the independent sales force, we recommend that Sales Directors concentrate 45 percent of their time on new people entering the business, 45 percent on their top performing people, and the remaining 10 percent on those who are on their way out of the business. It's the bottom 10 percent who account for the majority of problems and demand most of a Sales Director's time. These percentages are applicable to nearly all businesses, and good people leaders know that their time is more productively spent by developing both beginners and those with productive records behind them.

Determine Whether the Problem Is Valid

Of course, every problem must be examined to determine its validity. So again, I emphasize the importance of being a good listener. Find out if any verifiable facts exist or if the problem is simply manufactured or blown out of proportion. With a large independent sales force, if something is obviously wrong, we're likely to get strong feedback from many Independent Beauty Consultants and Sales Directors. This is especially true when a new product is introduced. For instance, when a new eyebrow pencil was marketed, many independent sales force members complained that it would break when it was sharpened. Our investigation revealed that the problem wasn't with the pencil, but with our sharpener. By changing to a double-edged sharpener, the point no longer broke off. Although we check out every single complaint, when so many women wrote to us about the eyebrow pencil, we *knew* immediately that the problem was real.

Merely because a large number of complaints are received, however, it shouldn't automatically be assumed that something is drastically wrong. Occasionally when we introduce a major change, the initial reaction is negative. We realize, however, that many people resist change—even change for the better. So while we always treat complaints seriously, after thorough investigation, we may discover that the change was justified. But it is how we communicate change that matters. It is advisable to carefully review beforehand your presentation of any contemplated change. It may be your presentation that is inadequate, not the change itself.

A Good Leader Listens Attentively for the *Real* Problem

There are people who complain because they want attention. They need an excuse to induce you to listen to them, so they come to you with an imagined problem. Hear them out, listen carefully, and you may be able to read between the lines and discover what's really bothering them—it could very well relate to that invisible sign I talked about in Chapter 3. Generally such conversations begin like this:

"Mary Kay, I've *got* to talk to you about a serious problem."

So an appointment is made and when the person comes in, she usually begins by apologizing, "Well actually, Mary Kay, I'm embarrassed to be taking up your time, but you see, well. . . . "

"Please tell me whatever it is that's troubling you," I say.

At this point I just sit back and listen and do a lot of nodding. Often, without my solving a single thing, the person ends the conversation by saying, "Mary Kay, I can't thank you enough for giving your valuable time to help me with this."

By the end of the conversation, it's obvious to me that this person didn't have a real problem. But she didn't know that—to her it was real. All she really needed was a little attention. Once she got it, her spirits were lifted and she went away feeling good about herself. Had I not given her that attention, she would have continued to believe that she had a problem. And believe me, *that* could have developed into something real.

A Leader Must Recognize When Home Problems Cause Work Problems

There are those people who rant and rave about a relatively minor problem when it's not the real issue at all. What that person is really reacting to has absolutely nothing to do with business. This happens quite frequently. Our experience indicates that the root cause—when a significant slump occurs—is often a problem unrelated to business. Often it's personal crises, such as those involving marriage, children, aging parents, family finances, and health, for example.

It has also been my observation that most women become more emotionally involved with interpersonal relationships, and they aren't as likely to be able to simply leave their personal problems at home. Yet we should not begrudge women this characteristic. It is the same trait that makes them sensitive and caring leaders.

I've read that women in the executive suite have a higher-than-average divorce rate. Some people believe that a successful businesswoman must neglect her family for her career. I don't believe this. Rather, I suspect that many "underemployed" women remain in unhappy marriages because of financial constraints. Once they obtain higher-paying jobs, a sense of financial independence gives them options. If this is true, then the divorce rate among female executives may not be as disturbing as it first appears.

Of course, some marital problems are directly related to double standards that have existed for many generations about a woman's career. For example, it's all right for a husband to have a demanding job that keeps him away from home until 10 or 11 P.M., as long as he calls his wife: "Honey, we're having an audit tonight; I won't be home until late," or "We're going to have to cancel that trip because I can't be away from the office that long," or "We can't go to that party you were so looking forward to." In our culture, such male prerogatives have always been acceptable. But let a woman call her husband with a similar message, and it's a different matter altogether. What is the remedy for such double standards? Primarily, I believe a woman must communicate to her spouse the nature of her work and the extent of her commitment to its success. She can gain his support only when he understands that her career goals are not a threat to their relationship or other obligations.

With the independent sales force, one way that we are able to enlist the support of spouses is by inviting them to attend our Company-sponsored events. When a Beauty Consultant or Sales Director brings her spouse, we invite him to attend special classes as well as recreational activities, such as bowling tourna-ments and golf outings. We've discovered that the more a spouse understands the nature of this business, the more supportive he will be. Once a husband understands his wife's goals, he's less likely to say, "For crying out loud, how long does a skin care class take anyway?" Instead, he's even willing to pitch in at home a few times a week when he recognizes how much it means to both his wife's self-development and to the family pocketbook. Without a spouse's support, people in any business can operate under handicaps that might otherwise drain even the strongest among us.

Discover Possible Solutions to the Problem

One important step in problem solving is to diagnose the exact nature of the problem. Here, too, the leader must work closely with his or her people. Tap this resource and ask them to help define the scope of the problem. During this analysis, consider this question: Are all elements of the problem within your (or your department's) jurisdiction?

If the problem comes from somewhere outside your control, can you change that pattern, institute corrective measures elsewhere, or adapt to the problem as it hits you? Let's imagine that you are the leader of a department that assembles a product made of parts that come from other companies. But something is wrong. The finished product does not work, and you've got a problem. You will diagnose the problem by analyzing each contributing part of the whole, by looking closely at the characteristics of each step in the assembly, and by carefully scrutinizing the end product. Eventually you recognize the problem: One of the components is too big. This discovery would lead you to the third step in problem solving: defining possible solutions.

The smart leader will once again use his other people in this phase of this process. A comfortable, free work environment will really pay dividends here, for this is where your people can take risks and devise creative solution possibilities. After much discussion, you and your staff determine that you could change suppliers, trim off some of the oversize part, or change the end product.

Often you're required to choose from among all possible options. If, in our hypothetical assembly operation, you learn that your workers may not change suppliers—nor can they shave off a few inches from the oversize component—then you may find that the best alternative is to enlarge the space in which that component is to be placed. In selecting the best alternative, of course, you must consider factors such as cost, time, use of personnel, and quality of the final product.

The next step in the problem-solving process is implementation. Here you may apply those provisions necessary to change that are discussed in Chapter 10. The last step is to follow through to make sure the problem has really been solved and to evaluate the quality of the "solution."

As a leader, you must be prepared to deal with a wide range of problems. Some will be real, some will be imagined, but most will be a combination of both. Listen to them all and keep an open mind. Finally—and perhaps most importantly—remember the old adage: "If it ain't broke, don't fix it."

Independent National Sales Directors Talk about Mary Kay Principles in Action Today

"Problems which are solved no longer block you. This frees you to take on new challenges," says **Rosemarie Sczech** of Germany, whose own daughter decided to join her mother in pursuing a Mary Kay business as soon as she turned 18.

"When you own your own business," says **Kathy Rasmussen** of the United States, "you must be willing to get out of your comfort zone. You must become skilled at solving problems and the buck stops with you."

"Women are good at having the gut feeling or intuition," says **Elizabeth Ozua**, who pioneered in the United Kingdom, and is now driving her sixth pink Mercedes. "When you combine that with the practice of praising to success and problem solving," she says, "you have a free environment for growth."

"It's a given that any business has problems of all kinds almost continuously," says **Wanda Janes** of the United States. "And I've always found the better equipped you are to solve the problems, the quicker you can help move things forward and the more successful you'll be."

21　Less Stress

A good leader minimizes stress for people. If a person is in the
midst of divorce proceedings or caring for a sick, elderly parent or
perhaps on the verge of declaring personal bankruptcy, it's a pretty
good guess that he or she is undergoing considerable stress.
Medical experts claim that severe stress can cause serious illnesses,
such as heart disease or cancer. Exactly how and to what extent
stress affects each individual is not fully understood. At the very
least, however, it is certain that stress can be highly destructive
both to the worker and to the employer. Thus every leader should
work to minimize stress in the workplace.

Please note, I didn't say "eliminate"; *some* stress is desirable—
even necessary. For instance, we all know that a long-distance run-
ner is likely to perform better under the impetus of strong competition. Or under the competitive pressure of a once-in-a-lifetime
opportunity, an Olympic skier or ice skater will set a world record.
Likewise, actors perform better before an audience than in an
empty rehearsal hall. To paraphrase John Barrymore, if you ever
lose the butterflies during a performance, you've lost your
audience. And I, both as a salesperson and as a speaker, have often
felt the flow of adrenaline, the body's normal reaction to stress. As
we all know, under certain conditions stress can heighten one's
performance. And so we don't want to eliminate it completely.
Rather we must recognize the different kinds of stress and the
various circumstances in which it may help us or hurt us.

Stress can be considered beneficial whenever a sense of urgency results in a superior performance. Some executives, for example, thrive on the excitement of being under pressure to get a "rush job" out on time. Others feel an exhilarating sense of tension from working with other highly talented people who challenge them to peak performance. Still others are stimulated to outdo themselves by the stress of a team effort, where an obligation to do one's best is combined with a fear of letting the team down. Such outstanding performances under the stimulus of stress are much admired because the results are positive and revitalizing.

A Friendly, Productive Environment Begins with You, the Leader

These kinds of stress work to our advantage, but another kind can be very destructive in business, undermining morale and productivity. As a leader, I believe in creating a friendly, relaxed working atmosphere. Life is too short to do otherwise. As I have said repeatedly, people perform better when they're happy and feel at ease with their leaders. Obviously, then, a friendly, productive atmosphere begins with you, the leader. Your moods directly affect the moods of those who report to you. A congenial leader will create less stress among his employees than will a dictatorial leader who enjoys criticizing people. I've worked for "dictators" who were always waiting to jump on you at the slightest provocation. I've worked in offices where the boss's temper tantrums would fill the room with so much tension that you could cut it with a knife. And I've worked in offices where the entire staff was so afraid to lift their eyes from their work that you could almost see the sweat on their foreheads. That's the kind of stress we can do without.

A leader usually has the authority to either fire an employee or determine his future within the department. An employee who has fallen out of favor with the boss can live in constant fear that he may be reprimanded, demoted, or even fired. This causes stress.

A working relationship of this nature offers no job security. I've been there, and I wouldn't wish it on anyone. For this reason, I make a strong effort to create exactly the opposite atmosphere— one in which people know that I sincerely care about their well-being. And as I have emphasized repeatedly in this book, when a leader cares about his or her people, the good feelings it engenders permeate the entire organization.

An Indecisive Leader Causes Stress in Others

I have observed that people feel more secure at work when they're supervised by a decisive leader. A leader who cannot confront a problem and make a decision causes stress among his people. A district sales manager for an office equipment company once confided to me, "Mary Kay, I'm completely frustrated in my job. The vice president of sales told me that my territory was doing poorly and said, 'I want it humming. Do what you must to get things moving.' He's never given me a quota, so I haven't the slightest idea what he expects the territory to produce. Nor do I know why he says we're slipping, since our sales volume has increased over the last year. My salespeople are doing well, and we're adequately servicing our existing accounts. I've asked him to be more specific, but he refuses to spell it out. He simply says, 'It's your job to decide what has to be done.'" No wonder this district sales manager felt frustrated and under great stress. When people are kept in the dark as to what's expected of them, anxiety takes over.

A Good Leader Provides Direction

People want strong leadership—leaders who give them a sense of direction. They feel comfortable with a leader who lets them know exactly what he wants and what's expected of them. Sometimes described by those who work for them as "tough," such leaders at least let you know where you stand. Of course there's such a thing as being too decisive—for example, a leader who comes across so strong that nobody dares disagree with him, even when he is obviously wrong. Under these circumstances employees back off from confrontation. "Once he makes up his mind," they'll say, "there's no sense in arguing with him. He's the boss and someone I never want to cross swords with." There's a big difference between a decisive leader and a tyrant.

There's also a big difference between being a leader who strives for excellence and being a rigid, uncompromising perfectionist. A perfectionist can exert undue pressure on his or her people, for no one can function well when placed under unrealistically high expectations. So while striving for excellence is admirable, failure must be tolerated in an imperfect world. It's unrealistic to always expect perfection. For this reason a leader should not set objectives that ask people to reach the unattainable.

Nor do I believe in imposing unrealistic deadlines. It's inconsiderate for a leader to assign a three-day workload to an employee and then to issue orders that it be finished the next day. I know the president of a large bank who's famous for waiting until the last moment to hand out major assignments that can't possibly be completed in the time he allows. His unrealistic deadlines subject his employees to a great deal of unnecessary stress.

A leader should also give clear, concise assignments. People become frustrated when they're merely told, "Do something about so-and-so."

"What do you want done?" the employee asks.

"Look, I can't spell it out for you—just take care of it, will you? I'm busy and don't have the time to spend with you," the leader fires back. Obviously, a vague or ambiguous order can create stress and reduce productivity.

An enormous amount of stress is endured by those who are promoted up the corporate ladder too quickly to positions they are not yet ready to assume. In my day many corporations that were previously guilty of this had gone overboard in crash efforts to rectify such errors. For this reason, I caution women, in particular, to avoid being cast in the role of the "token" woman manager. I've seen companies promote people to positions that were beyond their capabilities, thus causing them considerable stress. And in industries where barriers to women have only recently been lowered, the pressures are even greater. One woman, who had risen from accounting clerk to financial vice president of a major tool-and-die company in a brief six-year period, said to me, "I'm on the verge of a nervous breakdown, Mary Kay. At least four men under me are more capable, but my company needed a woman in the executive suite, and I happened to be the only female candidate. I feel as though the male leaders in the company resent my promotion. Sometimes I think they're all just standing by, waiting for me to fail. The job is over my head, I'll admit, but if I resign, I'll be out on the street looking for employment. So when I'm not at the office, I've been spending my spare evenings doing my homework. Initially, my husband and kids were supportive, but now they've just about had it. The pressure is getting to me both on and off the job."

I've also seen that some leaders try too hard to emulate executives. In the process, personality changes frequently occur. It's not uncommon to hear such remarks as "She never smiles anymore,"

or "He seems to have lost his sense of humor," or "I never realized
what a temper she has, but lately, she's quick to fly off the
handle." To be accepted as "one of the boys," some newly
promoted managers will start to use profanity, and this can result
in the loss of respect of both their male and female associates. I
personally never use profanity, and because I don't, those around
me don't either. Frankly, I don't think many women feel
comfortable using coarse language—nor do they respect those
people who do. It's demeaning for anyone to speak in a way that
doesn't come naturally. When women managers emulate men in
order to gain acceptance, undue stress is bound to result. But
being her own person is the most effective way for a woman to
move up the corporate ladder. As such, she brings a welcome new
dimension to the executive suite.

Change Can Bring on Stress

Change, whether good or bad, is yet another major contributing
cause of stress. Practically every psychologist will tell you that
some people can become seriously ill from stress brought on by a
major change—the death of a loved one, a divorce, or the loss of
job, for example. Even a happy occasion such as marriage may
bring on stress that can cause a health problem. No matter what
the nature of the change, it may result in stress for some people.
With this in mind, change should be implemented gradually, giving your people ample time to adjust to it. And whenever possible
they should be involved in the early stages. Remember: People will
support that which they help to create. Whenever we make any
kind of change affecting the independent sales force—revisions
in commission schedules, price increases, education, or team-
building techniques—we give notice in advance so that everyone
has plenty of time to adjust.

We have always worked hard to create a less stressful atmosphere for our people, and we take action to bring it about. We do this by letting everyone know that every leader is available when someone has a problem. Furthermore, we encourage any troubled employee to "talk it out." I believe that if an individual is under a great deal of stress, the first thing to do is to confront the issue. Left unattended, problems only intensify.

People often say to me, "Mary Kay, in your present position—with so much responsibility—you must have far greater stress than you did back in the early days of your career." While many people seem to believe that the amount of stress an individual encounters increases in direct proportion to his or her responsibilities, I disagree. For me the stress was far greater when I had to worry about having enough money to put food on the table, pay the rent, and buy clothes for my children. The insecurities I endured from those uncertainties were far greater than those I now encounter in the executive suite. And although it has been years since we started our business, I haven't forgotten what it was like to endure that kind of stress. I believe every leader would do well to remember his or her early "pre-management days." It helps to put things in truer perspective, and you can understand from your own experience the stress-related problems of those who work for you.

Independent National Sales Directors Talk about Mary Kay Principles in Action Today

"When I first learned about Mary Kay, I didn't believe it was for me. I thought it was for the American woman. As I learned more, I realized that it is possible to thoroughly enjoy our work. I always teach," says **Monica Medina Oliver** of Argentina, "that work should not be a stress or sacrifice, but a source of happiness. And we should pass this idea to our families."

"As women working from what are mostly home-based businesses, stress can come from bad habits or poor organization. Mary Kay believed from the very beginning that we needed to establish business hours—even though they might be staggered—and develop guidelines to work around the parameters of our families. If we could honor both of these, we wouldn't make the most common mistake, failing to get organized," said **Eddie Howley-Beggrow** of the United States.

"No one flourishes under constant pressure. It's bad for your mind and health," says **Mary Diem** of the United States, who has found great satisfaction in the role of encourager and cheerleader to women.

"The only way to be self-motivated is to be self-disciplined. One of the greatest stress reducers is a little tool I still rely upon. It's Mary Kay's Six Most Important Things list." says **Wynne Lou Ferguson** of the United States of the practice of prioritizing before leaving your office for the day, the *next* day's six most important tasks. "Learning to use this is the first step necessary when we are self-employed. Because we are in business for ourselves, we must be self-motivated and self-disciplined."

22 Develop People from Within

At Mary Kay Inc. we believe in promoting people from within the Company. An outsider is normally not brought in if we already employ a person who is qualified. Whenever a position is open, the department manager formally submits the job description to be posted so those qualified may apply. It doesn't matter which job that employee may already have. If someone is unhappy in her present job, feels the new job is a promotion opportunity, and thinks she may be qualified, she may apply. Every interested employee will be interviewed, and sometimes as many as 25 people apply for a single position. Only after all employee applicants have been interviewed and given careful consideration do we go outside the Company to fill the position. In many cases the job will go to one of our own people; the exceptions are usually highly specialized professional jobs such as chemists, microbiologists, or lawyers.

This system works extremely well for us. It's interesting to observe how employees' responsibilities and salaries increase over the years.

Such opportunities for individual growth create a healthy climate that encourages employees to think in terms of a long career with the Company. Thus it is clear to those just beginning that they don't have to stay in one position forever. It gives hope to someone working 40 hours a week at a capping machine that he won't be there five years hence unless he wants to be. A packer in the warehouse, a manager in accounting, or a computer programmer can find other work within the Company if he's unhappy at his present position. If he's willing to sharpen his skills and increase his knowledge of how the Company operates, there are many other positions available. It's just a matter of looking around for the jobs for which he is qualified. This system reduces turnover to a minimum. After spending months training an employee to be productive on a job, we feel that losing him is too costly.

The system also has a domino effect. For instance, when a managerial position opens up, fourteen people may apply for it. After someone is chosen, that person's job is sought by eighteen other people. And when *it's* filled, perhaps someone fills the second job, and so on. Move one piece on the board, and five or six more moves will follow. As one job is filled, other vacancies are created down the line.

We often cross-train people so that they are capable of doing several jobs—not one. Thus it is easier for someone to be already qualified in several areas. On the packaging floor in manufacturing, for example, all workers are rotated regularly from job to job so that eventually everyone can perform any job in the department. The boredom of doing the same repetitive job day after day, year after year, is thereby eliminated. Absenteeism is also reduced, and when someone is ill, we have the flexibility of rotating work assignments. Within a year, a new employee on the packaging floor in manufacturing can work his way through several jobs in the department and develop a reasonable level of competency at each job. If the person assigned to the capping machine is absent for a period of time, we can assign someone else to the task. Without a backup system of this kind, we could face serious production problems. For instance, imagine the downtime a flu epidemic could create if several key workers were out at once and no one could do their jobs.

Today, Mary Kay develops, tests, manufactures, and packages most of its products in our state-of-the-art U.S. manufacturing facility located in Dallas. This facility has 430,000 square feet, 35 processing vessels, and 27 packaging lines that are capable of producing approximately 1 million units per day. Production lines operate 24 hours a day, six days a week; and commitment to safety and quality excellence is our No. 1 priority. In 2006, Mary Kay opened a second manufacturing plant in China, producing products for consumers in the region.

A Good Leader Trains Her Replacement

For a leader to be promoted, there should be a backup person to replace her. Every leader realizes that her advancement depends in part upon how well she trains others to take over her present position. Let's face it; if there's no one who can step into that leader's shoes, we can't very well promote her. Every leader must realize therefore that no one in the Company is indispensable. And the person who tries to make himself indispensable by not training his replacement has, in reality, made his own promotion unlikely and backed himself into a corner. The essence of good organizational development is a leadership team that recognizes the importance of developing the competence of those who must eventually assume their jobs. And the better those people are the more credit the leader deserves! Of course, there are sometimes those with egos that get in their way. Perhaps due to insecurities, they become fearful about developing a replacement. But how shortsighted they are not to realize that in our Company restricting another's advancement severely limits their own.

Seek Out Assistance at Every Level

Experienced employees are extremely helpful to any leader. I think it's wise to let such a person know her value: "I need your help; in fact, I can't do my job effectively without you." It's never a bad idea to seek out other experienced co-workers to assist you. At the same time, a leader should set competency goals for herself and perhaps take extra classes in related subjects to sharpen her overall skills.

I have sometimes been asked whether I think a woman should pass up a promotion by admitting that she can't face the pressures of the job. If the job is very far beyond her capacity, I'd have to say yes. But in most cases, the promotion is not beyond her true ability. Using patience, honesty, and hard work, women can find others willing to help.

Let's hope all companies realize that there are many talented women in their organizations, and that these women represent a largely untapped leadership resource. Perhaps when they do they will pay particular attention to that quality often called "woman's intuition" and welcome the new insight it can bring to the executive suite. Although in the past it was considered an elusive quality, cognitive scientists and learning specialists now recognize intuition as a highly developed thought process. Rather than simply "appearing from the blue," intuition is actually quite logical. It is the observation, synthesis, and recollection of countless patterns in human behavior. Someone "intuitively" knows something because he or she can accurately predict reasonable consequences. And in my experience, women are more skillful than men in this regard. They seem to intuitively know how other people will feel and react.

In a well-run company that offers equal advancement opportunities to all employees, the cream always rises to the top. In fact, a recent study of the best-managed companies in America shows that they are structured in a way that *guarantees* the best people will be promoted to top levels of management. I view it as a sign of weakness when a company fails to develop a leadership team from within. Nothing prepares one better for the responsibilities of leadership than on-the-job training.

Build with People from Within the Organization

In the independent sales force, every person starts out equal as an Independent Beauty Consultant. There are never any exceptions. In 1967, four years after we started the Company, a group of businessmen offered us $100,000 for an exclusive franchise for Birmingham, Alabama. Although at the time that was a great deal of money, we turned them down. On another occasion several managers from a defunct competitor approached us, asking for key positions in the independent sales force. They wanted to start as Sales Directors, but we informed them that they would have to begin in the field like everyone else—as Beauty Consultants.

"But, Mary Kay," they said, "we've been recruiting, training, and managing salespeople for more years than you've been in business."

"If you're as good as you say," I explained, "it will only take you about six months to learn our product, our philosophy, and our marketing plan. Then you can begin to build and educate your own units. But it would wreck the morale of the independent sales force to bring in outsiders as Sales Directors." These women weren't willing to begin as Beauty Consultants, and even though they seemed very competent, we refused to accept their proposal. I know another direct-sales company that was once offered $50,000 for a franchise in their best city. The company's president told the manager of that territory either to meet that offer or the franchise would be sold. The manager, who happened to be the company's top sales manager, was devastated and quit. When word of what had happened got out to the sales organization, almost everyone else also resigned. For a direct-sales company, there is no substitute for building with people from within.

The same approach applies to every healthy company; everyone must know that the measure of advancement is individual performance. They must be secure in the knowledge that if they excel, they deserve to be promoted and will be. By the same token, they must realize that as their value to the company increases, the company itself grows, because without growth, opportunities for advancement are limited. There is an old saying that goes "When you are growing, green you are, but when you are ripe, you are rotten." A business cannot stagnate. When growth ceases, a company can't offer new job opportunities unless people quit or retire! In such an environment, the people most likely to stay with a company are those who are the least productive.

Good people need opportunities and challenges. That's what causes excitement and keeps a company humming at a fast pace. Every leader should have the feeling that he's at the right place at the right time. You can evaluate your own circumstances by asking yourself this simple question: After a full night's sleep, do you rise refreshed and eager to tackle an interesting problem or a brand-new idea? Or do you drag out of bed and begrudgingly prepare for "another day at the grindstone"? If you experience the latter, chances are that you have an inappropriate, perhaps even dreary job. But if you experience the former, you not only have the right attitude, you also have an exciting career opportunity.

Independent National Sales Directors Talk about Mary Kay Principles in Action Today

"What is important about this Company is that each person brings goodness, and the goodness spreads," says **Irina Maniak** of Russia, who was a young mother working on her dissertation at a St. Petersburg university when she attended a Mary Kay skin care class. "This happens every day in every city and every country. I have many team members across enormous Russia, and when we get together, there is an incredible relationship between these women and their families; between these women and their customers." Because Mary Kay believed in building others up and bringing them along to become leaders, Irina has seen a philosophy of "everyone bringing goodness. Mary Kay never knew me but she has dramatically changed my life."

For **Maria Monarrez** of the United States, it was a promise she made to Mary Kay "that I would always drive a pink Cadillac" that spurred her on to see "that what you do for others will come back to you in a positive way in the future. Where I lived, schooling ended after sixth grade, so I was sent to live with my aunt to continue my studies." With a university degree, she learned to instill self-confidence in women she met, finding joy in helping others better their lifestyle just as she did.

"I learned from Mary Kay to believe in people before they believed in themselves," says **Donna Floberg** of the United States. "In leading by example and taking others with me to the top, I would explain there is no elevator in Mary Kay, but that with a few steps forward at a time, they could get there as fast as they wanted."

23 Live by the Golden Rule On and Off the Job

I truly believe that the Golden Rule was intended to be used seven days a week—not just on Sunday. And that it should be employed in every relationship—business or personal. When you use this rule, every decision becomes a right decision.

I believe you must apply its principles on and off the job. If compassion and fair dealing are good for business, why not practice those same excellent qualities away from the office—at home, for example? Keeping your priorities as God first, family second, and career third somehow keeps life in harmony. While everyone is uniquely valuable as a person, the most important people in our lives are our families and friends.

Yet all too often we neglect our loved ones, taking them for granted because they're always there—in the morning when we leave for work and in the evening when we return home. Some women give no thought to their appearance when they're around their husbands and children, even though these are the most important people in their lives. Most of their "dressing up" is for strangers. Shouldn't it be the other way around? And, of course, most men are also guilty of this, caring more about their appearance in the eyes of their co-workers than their families.

It's easy to get so caught up in our work that we ignore our families. It takes effort to be attentive. Are we too tired to make that effort for our families? "Why bother?" you say. "They accept me the way I am." But should they have to? How many business people spend most of their working day on the telephone and at meetings and then barely speak to their spouse and children when they return home? Recently a man complained to me about his wife, a marketing executive: "Jane's a nonstop talker with everyone else all day long, but at home she rarely talks to me. And she doesn't even seem to hear a thing I say to her. 'Honey,' she says, 'you're the only person I can be with and just be myself.'"

Obviously, she didn't get the message her husband was sending: "I feel neglected and unloved." I know what it's like to be exhausted after a full day's work, but I think that her husband deserves the same courtesies she extends to her co-workers at the office. Yes, it takes effort, but that's the price for successful personal relationships away from the job as well as at work.

As it requires effort to communicate with your business associates, it also requires effort to communicate with your spouse. Have you ever noticed married couples in a restaurant who eat without saying a word, hardly looking at each other? Or one of them does all the talking while the other seems not to hear a word. And every now and then the talker reprimands the other: "Will you please listen to me? You haven't heard a word I've said!"

Remember that invisible sign: Everyone needs to feel important. And no one counts more than your loved ones! They, too, wear an invisible sign. They, too, need praise. You know how valuable it is to tell an employee "You did a great job on the XYZ account. Keep up the good work." Your family is no different.

They crave the same pat on the back and will respond accordingly. When they deserve praise, don't withhold it: "Honey, that roast beef was delicious tonight," or "Matthew, I just read your term paper, and it's terrific. I'm proud of you, son," or "Jennifer, I know you're disappointed about losing the tennis match today, but I thought you played as well as I've ever seen you play. There's no disgrace in losing when you've done your best, and if you continue playing that well, I know you'll win a lot more matches." All you have to do is look around; there's never a lack of reason to praise members of your family. And when you do, you'll make their day. Remember that brief note you left the janitor: "You gave that floor such a high polish last night, I could see my reflection in it. Many thanks." When's the last time you left a similar note for someone at home?

Many of us also have a tendency to be overly critical of our loved ones. Again, we should extend the same patience and courtesy to them that we do to our co-workers. A little tact at home goes a long way. We would all do well to sandwich every bit of criticism between two thick layers of praise: "Johnny, you're much too bright to get a D in math. It disappoints me too see your grades slip, because I know you have the ability to be an outstanding student. For the rest of this semester, I want to see you studying at least two hours every night. I know if you apply yourself, you'll do well." Then give the child a hug and a kiss. Again it's the "sandwich" technique.

Everything that you do to become a good leader is also good advice when you're away from the job. For instance, "the speed of the leader is the speed of the gang" is a sentiment that is applicable in the home too. The father who tries to rally his children to pitch in with the spring housecleaning will get much more cooperation and enthusiasm if he starts by rolling up his own sleeves rather than by ordering everyone else around.

And "people will support that which they help to create" is a rule that works away from the office as well as in it.

One summer, a friend of mine took her three teenage children to Europe. She enlisted their help in planning the entire trip. They were to visit three countries—England, France, and Italy—and so she made each child responsible for planning the itinerary of one country. Each child went to the library to research the historical sites to be visited in "his" country. Then for several weeks before the actual trip, family discussions were conducted to set the agenda for each day of the vacation. This mother was wise to solicit her children's participation. She could have planned the entire itinerary with a travel agent, and it would have been considerably easier, but had she done so, her children would probably have been far less enthusiastic and knowledgeable about the trip. By participating in the planning of the trip, they all agreed that it was their best vacation ever.

A parent also shouldn't hide behind a policy with children. Consider, for instance, if a 15-year-old daughter who has been invited to her first dance is told by her father to be home by 11:30 P.M.

"But why so early?" she asks. "The dance won't be over until 1 A.M."

"You heard me. Be home by 11:30."

"But why?"

"Because I said so. I make the rules around here. You can do what you want with *your* kids. But in my house I'm the boss."

"You're treating me like a baby," she cries.

"I'll treat you any way I want. I'm your father."

Unfortunately, this little scenario is all too common. We need to be reminded every so often not to dictate to our children but to direct, coach and educate them.

Perhaps your parents were tyrants, and for that reason you feel you have the right to treat your children the same way. But just because it was that way when you were growing up doesn't mean it's right today. Young people will say, "Times are different now," and they're right. Times *are* different today. We must learn to deal with social change as well as changes in the business and professional world.

We've discussed stress in the workplace, but it's by no means confined to the office or shop. Stress is all around us, and most of it can be reduced. To reduce it, you must first be aware of those problems that cause stress. Too often we shut our eyes to problems, hoping they will disappear. Instead of bottling up feelings, healthy families express them, which in itself can reduce stress.

A person, for example, might enjoy his or her role so much at the office in comparison to life at home that they feel guilty about it. They may know how to cope with stress at work, but they feel pressures in their personal life. Perhaps being behind the wheel in hectic traffic while chauffeuring a carload of noisy children takes its toll on their nerves. Or it may be that when he or she entertains a houseful of company they feel stress caused by wondering about people's reactions to the preparations. On top of the workload at the office, he or she may feel the pressure of not having enough hours in the day to get the house in order. It's necessary to get your life synchronized on and off the job, because if you can't manage your personal responsibilities, they may very well affect your work. You can't live two separate lives. You must put your whole act together!

Throughout this book, many suggestions have been made about working effectively with people by using my self-taught style of Golden Rule leadership. Although few people ever thought it could be applied in business, we have proved that it can be—and it's workable! There is no patent on it; what has worked for us will also work for you. But it will work only if it's coupled with integrity and conviction. You can't fake living by the Golden Rule because people sense insincerity immediately. You must earn the unconditional respect of the people you work with. And, of course, you will be judged by your behavior away from the job as well as by your 9-to-5 conduct. No one functions well under double standards. No one can serve two masters.

While the purpose of this book is to increase your leadership skills in working with people, it is my hope that you won't limit its usefulness to the office. Don't be so deeply involved in your work that you neglect those who are closest to you—your family and friends. With your priorities clearly established, the best part of life will not elude you. Finally, I would like to wish for each one of you a full life—one that enriches the lives of everyone around you.

Independent National Sales Directors Talk about Mary Kay Principles in Action Today

"More than anything else, we learned the intangibles by watching Mary Kay Ash lead. Her teachings have followed me throughout life," says **Doretha Dingler** of the United States, the first to earn $100,000 in commissions in a single month. "She was able to bring out the 'jewel' in each of us. Mary Kay treated people the way she wanted to be treated, and left them feeling like a million bucks."

"Our area has been terrific at extending to area members during challenging times. Because of Mary Kay's influence, we send care notes, donate time and money, and most of all, we live a life of giving. We learned this from Mary Kay herself," says **Judie McCoy** of the United States.

Rosa Jackson of the United States saw this chapter put into action. In 1969 she was studying for a master's degree in religious education while her husband completed seminary studies in Atlanta, GA. When Mary Kay Ash learned of difficulties Rosa faced building her business, "that's when Mary Kay personally got involved. She became my cheering section. Over the course of our talks about prejudice, she apologized for our society. She told me, 'I believe we are all equal in the sight of God. You can go to the top with your business, so don't let a few narrow-minded people discourage you."

Afterword

Leaders Creating Leaders:
Mary Kay's Living Legacy

People constantly ask where I get my inspiration and motivation. It's from National Sales Directors, who have attained the epitome of what I would hope that all of the independent sales force will become. One of these days, I will pass the torch to you, and it will be your responsibility to take our Company to greater heights than ever. I know that I have not misplaced my faith. Thank you for being so wonderful. Thank you for your leadership and your belief in our Company, and thank you for what you are doing to help thousands and thousands of other women achieve the same success that you enjoy.

—*Mary Kay Ash 1993 speech to National Sales Directors*

When she began preparing to write a book on her business principles, Mary Kay had no idea that her cornerstone values and principles would be considered revolutionary by some business leaders and "quaint" by others. But she was certain was that these principles worked. By the time this book was first published in 1984, Mary Kay had an established 20-year track record running her own business according to The Mary Kay Way, in addition to 25 prior years working for other companies. She had fully experienced the frustration of being a working mother with no role models and little opportunity for advancement. At that time, no one in the business world had any inkling of what was to come if and when the minds and hearts of its women were engaged. If Mary Kay understood anything, it was the possibilities in store for women. She knew that once they had a success path in place, women would be great achievers. Many of the top-level Mary Kay National Sales Directors marvel at how she believed in them long before they believed in themselves.

Mary Kay Ash passed away in 2001. But her values and principles continue to attract people around the world to her unusual company. Today over 1.8 million women are independent sales people for Mary Kay, and Mary Kay® products are sold in more than 35 markets worldwide.

Mary Kay's son and Company co-founder Richard Rogers, executive chairman of Mary Kay Inc., paid homage to these women and particularly the leaders in the independent sales force at the Company's annual Seminar in his first public address after Mary Kay's death:

> Mary Kay knew what she had started was larger than her life. Enriching women's lives around the world would not end when her life ended. She knew we would need the leadership of those who believed in her dream. Those who would commit to carry on her principles and beliefs.

> My mother was smart. But I don't think even she could conceive that so many women would earn the title of National Sales Director in her lifetime. You are the first of many generations of leaders to carry her torch throughout the world, to give meaning to her life in a new century. At mother's Memorial Service, I looked to the left of where I was sitting, and as far as my eyes could see, there you were—honoring Mary Kay with your own

loving memories of her. Leaders and role models in your own right, strong and capable and genuine—for all the world to see the Mary Kay legacy in you.

—*Richard R. Rogers*

In addition to a much-celebrated culture, Mary Kay Ash created an organizational system in which leaders continually mentor new leaders within the independent sales force. Her concept of "leaders creating leaders" has been studied for many years by academics. It eventually became a kind of succession plan. For the Mary Kay independent sales force, National Sales Directors today provide the role modeling, motivation, and inspiration that Mary Kay herself embodied in the early years of the Company. National Sales Directors are the top achievers among the millions of women who've established Mary Kay businesses.

By instilling her principles in these leaders, Mary Kay remained influential and critical to the success of the Company, long after her active tenure at the Company.

For example, when the original edition of this book, titled *On People Management*, was published in 1984, there were 60 Mary Kay National Sales Directors—all of them in the United States. It would be seven more years before a National Sales Director would debut in a Mary Kay international subsidiary, but today more than half the Independent National Sales Directors reside in the global markets. More than 500 women entrepreneurs around the world have now become National Sales Directors, and they credit Mary Kay's own simple roadmap with helping them reach this extremely high level of achievement. In cultures, nations, and languages far removed from her native Texas roots, the National Sales Directors now provide a living, working, role modeling laboratory for generations who never had the chance to know Mary Kay personally.

One example of Mary Kay's leadership style with her National Sales Directors was in the writing of this book. She wanted to make sure it reflected not just her own ideas, but also the experiences of the first generation of company leaders. So in the early 1980s, she invited a dozen or so top National Sales Directors to come to Dallas to discuss what had been their reality—the practical application of her principles in their own lives and careers.

Ann Sullivan, a National Sales Director Emeritus who built her Mary Kay business in Missouri, was one of those invited to the idea exchange. "Mary Kay was a master at sharing ideas. She asked us to write down the things that had been instrumental for us in building our businesses around her principles. She wanted very much for us to share anything that would be helpful to others who were following in our footsteps. Then we discussed all the ideas. That really is the essence of her genius. Many ideas shared and multiplied over time."

The People in the Principles
Leadership the Mary Kay Way

A great believer in simplicity, Mary Kay also synthesized the 23 chapters in her original book into eight statements she called her Leadership Principles (see page 225). Some might see this as a "Cliff's Notes" type version of the wisdom in this book. That wouldn't have bothered Mary Kay Ash at all—the important thing for her was that she be very clear so people would have no trouble grasping these concepts.

In our surveys of Independent National Sales Directors, three of these eight Leadership Principles continually surfaced as having the most impact—most likely for their emphasis on people and the priorities that decidedly shaped the Company from its very beginning.

The Eight Principles

1. Praise People to Success
Recognition is the most powerful of all motivators. Even criticism can build confidence when it's "sandwiched" between layers of praise.

2. Tear Down That Ivory Tower
Be accessible to all. And listen.

3. Be a Risk-Taker
And encourage your teams to take risks too.

4. Be Sales-Oriented
Be sensitive to your customers' needs and desires.

5. Be a Problem-Solver
Recognize real problems and take action.

6. Create a Stress-Free Workplace
Inspire increased productivity.

7. Develop and Promote People from Within
You'll build loyalty.

8. Keep Business in its Proper Place
And learn this is the real key to success.

The three most critical are:

Praise People to Success

Develop and Promote People from Within

Keep Business in its Proper Place

An overwhelming 60 percent named Praise People as having the greatest influence on their careers, agreeing with Galina Kiseleva of Russia, the No. 1 National Sales Director in the Europe region, who said:

> This book is perfect proof that praise and encouragement are vital not only for private life, but for business as well. When you praise people, you touch their personal interest and their sphere of personal growth. In business it can have a direct, positive impact on the results of their work. Praising people creates a fruitful atmosphere that in turn creates self-confidence.

Another uniquely Mary Kay precept for leadership—and the second most influential of the eight—also follows the people principle. Not surprisingly, it gets at the root of the Mary Kay philosophy of leaders creating leaders.

Nan Jiang of China, the No. 1 National Sales Director in the Asia-Pacific region, described the principle Develop and Promote People from Within in this way:

> Mary Kay once said that leadership begins with the heart, not the head. It is difficult to develop and promote others if we don't believe in, appreciate, respect, and understand the Mary Kay Way. Mary Kay is the one who taught me that leadership begins with the heart, not the head. Her philosophy is her gift.

Third among the most-mentioned of Mary Kay business principles is an extension of Mary Kay's "God first, family second, career third" philosophy. The powerful impact of this principle—Keep Business in its Proper Place—cannot be understated among a group of focused, career-minded, successful businesswomen. Or as Mara de los Angeles D'Acosta de

De Anda of Mexico, the No. 1 National Sales Director in the Latin Americas region, put it:

> When I discovered that Mary Kay wasn't just a business but also a set of guiding philosophies for business and life, I fell in love with the Company. Mary Kay's philosophy of God first, family second, career third was one of her most significant legacies. She showed us that the path toward a fulfilled life comes from helping others achieve fulfilled lives. It's very satisfying to be able to make a positive influence on the lives of so many women while keeping life's priorities in order.

The Most Influential Book Chapters

As for the actual 23 chapters in the book, National Sales Directors we surveyed were united in the belief that each one was important. Moreover, they view the chapters as building blocks that help internalize the total message. There were, however, four that were consistently mentioned as having greatest personal impact. Interestingly enough, each of the four speaks volumes about the Mary Kay Ash and the way her message resonates among women.

Those four chapters are:

The essence of Mary Kay's philosophy:
Chapter 12: Help Other People Get What They Want—and You'll Get What You Want

The cornerstone of her legacy:
Chapter 1: Golden Rule Management

The unique recognition of others:
Chapter 3: The Invisible Sign

Her hands-on leadership style:
Chapter 9: The Speed of the Leader Is the Speed of the Gang

Something Mary Kay had learned as a young businesswoman made such an impression she never forgot it and urged everyone to practice it: "The Invisible Sign." At the time of her death in 2001, as the media accolades poured forth from around the world, one business school MBA candidate wrote a letter to Mary Kay thanking her for the valuable lesson inherent in this "invisible sign" philosophy. The letter was printed on the op-ed page of a prominent newspaper. The graduate student told how much better the MBA peer evaluations had become since the class had adopted Mary Kay's "make me feel important" mantra. Taking another page from Mary Kay, these graduate students had even been inspired to applaud each other's presentations.

Mary Kay's favorite response when someone asked her what her goals were after she was so famous was, "It's a good day if just one more woman finds out how great she really is."

Conclusion: Leaders Creating Leaders

The Independent National Sales Director who currently holds the No. 1 position in the world, Barbara Sunden of the United States, described the role of National Sales Directors today.

> Our leadership is a reflection of our Founder—her influence on others, her belief in others, and her vision for a greater future. There is a certain way of doing things, and for us, that is The Mary Kay Way. We learned how to conduct our business from Mary Kay Ash herself. We watched her, listened to her, and learned from her practical wisdom. For those among us who never had the privilege of knowing Mary Kay personally, we serve today as role models who present a true model of The Mary Kay Way of doing business.

> Whenever Mary Kay taught us how to reach out to our new team members, she would say:

> Tell them how you do it.

> Show them how you do it.

Let them show you how they do it.

She believed, as is so often said, that more is caught than taught. How true. And how necessary.

It's very true that so many of Mary Kay's principles have been "caught" by women whose lifestyles and languages are vastly different. And their real meaning can be summed up in the words of a woman in Kazakhstan who never met Mary Kay Ash. Independent National Sales Director Valentina Munatayeva described feeling a deep sense of obligation to carry on and pass forward Mary Kay's legacy:

> Her wisdom is simple and deep. My task is to become a mediator of Mary Kay's wisdom for the Beauty Consultants. A great puzzle comes together from small, beautiful pieces.

Index

and listening, 191–192

personal testimonies,
195–196

validity of problem,
190–191

R

Rasmussen, Kathy, 195

Raynor, Mary Pat, 187

Rockefeller, John D., 23

Rogers, Richard, xvii, xviii

Romanova, Elena, 79

Ross, Pam, 166

S

Safer, Morley, xv

"Sandwich technique," 51

Santin, Jean, 114

Schwab, Charles, 63–64

Sczech, Rosemarie, 195

Segal, Brenda, 28

Self-improvement:

and "executivitis," 148–149,
183–183, 184

and knowledge, 146–146

learning from others,
149–150, 208–209

personal testimonies, 152

program for, 145–146

and sharing ideas, 150–151

Seminar, 31–33

Shaw, Pamela Waldrop, 56

Shershneva, Liliya, 37

Silchenko, Nadezhda, 12

Six Most Important Things, 64

60 Minutes, xv

Sloan, Alfred, 19

Steinman, Sherril, xxii

Stoker, Angie, 12

Stoops, Carol, 56

Stroud, Nan, 123

Sullivan, Ann, 224

Sullivan, Nancy, 80

Sunden, Barbara, 228

T

Tang, Ke, 144

Tarbet, Rena, 114

Thomson, Erma, 109

Turner-Allen, Norelle, 47

W

Ward, Carolyn, 105

Warfield, Cheryl, 36

"We Heard You" program,
57–58